M000251149

the definitive guide to cooking

GRAINS

seeds & legumes

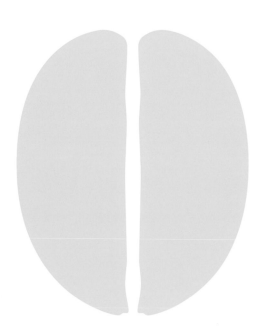

150 recipes for every appetite

MOLLY BROWN
PHOTOGRAPHY BY DEIRDRE ROONEY

Introduction

Whole grains, pulses, legumes and seeds have long suffered from an image problem. They have been eaten, or so it seems, by those more concerned with health than with flavour. The fact that they were good for you seemed to mean that consuming them was a penance rather than a pleasure. And many of us have failed to cook them with any kind of understanding or verve.

A plateful of boiled beans, unseasoned and unflavoured, is not going to excite anyone's taste buds. Yet grains, pulses, legumes and seeds are widely used in the most exciting cuisines. Cooks in the Middle East, Morocco, India, Italy and Spain don't cook with these ingredients because they're healthy; they do so because they're an integral part of their culinary tradition. It's hard to cling to the idea that lentils are dull if you eat them cooked the Indian way – thick with coconut milk and scented with cardamom and coriander. It is impossible to think that burghul (bulgur wheat) is just beige pap when faced with a platter of kisir, a Turkish dish of burghul flavoured with cumin, garlic, parsley and pomegranate molasses, rich with tomatoes and olive oil. Our relatively recent exposure to the cuisines of other countries has gone a long way to making us embrace grains, pulses, legumes and seeds in a way we never have before. But we've only really dipped our toes in the water.

I have never wanted to eat healthy food as a matter of course – I am pretty greedy and I want to eat food because it's gorgeous. But when I looked more closely at the health benefits of these ingredients I was astonished. These foods are delicious and good for you. I started to try things I had never considered before: tiny, nutrition-packed chia seeds are easy to add to muesli and breads, and they contain more omega-3 fatty acids than salmon. Wholemeal (whole-wheat) grains were also a revelation – they make a nutty and sweet salad base and are also chock-full of protein, potassium, iron, calcium and vitamins. I made my own granola and started looking forward to breakfast when I was going to bed. I had to make a little bit more effort in terms of organisation – if a grain or bean needed to be soaked overnight I had to remember to do it. But many of these ingredients can be cooked in advance and sit happily in the refrigerator until I want to turn them into something wonderful.

The dishes in this book are very good for you. By slightly altering your outlook and opening your mind about what you are prepared to try, they are easy to include in your cooking repertoire. But the best thing about incorporating these healthy foods into your cooking is that they are absolutely delicious. Just have a go. The proof of the pudding is in the eating ...

SEEDS

PUMPKIN SEEDS

Pumpkin seeds (pepitas) are delicious toasted and can be sprinkled on bread and cakes or mixed into dough or batter. They are also good scattered over salads. In autumn when cooking with pumpkin you can remove the seeds, separate them from the fibres and dry them in a 150°C (300°F) oven – salt them or coat them in spices beforehand if desired. It's also possible to make pale green milk from pumpkin seeds. Blitz them with water – about 1 litre (34 fl oz/4 cups) water to 150 g (5½ oz/1 cup) seeds – then squeeze the mixture through muslin (cheesecloth) and collect the 'milk'. Use this in soups or sweeten it and add to smoothies. The seeds can also be made into luscious green oil, particularly popular in Austria for salad dressings. Pumpkin seeds are suitable for sprouting.

FULL OF:
protein, manganese, magnesium, iron, zinc and phosphorus

SUNFLOWER KERNELS

Sunflower kernels can be bought shelled (small and beige) or unshelled (black and beige). Add them to bread dough, muesli and cereals, or sprinkle on salads. You can also make milk (see Pumpkin seeds for method). Sunflower oil is one of the most used cooking oils in the world. Its light flavour is probably the reason for its popularity, as it doesn't interfere with other elements in a dish. It is also considered to be very healthy as it combines monounsaturated and polyunsaturated fats, and has low levels of saturated fat. The oil's mild flavour also makes it useful in dressings where you want other flavours to dominate, for example, in South-East Asian dressings containing rice vinegar, soy and ginger. They are also suitable for sprouting.

FULL OF:
manganese, magnesium, phosphorus, folic acid, vitamin E and vitamins B6 and B1

LINSEEDS

Linseeds, also known as flax seeds, are slightly larger than sesame seeds with colours ranging from deep amber to reddish-brown. Because they are small it's easy to add them to foods such as bread, muesli, granola or pikelets (griddle cakes) without their flavour being too intrusive. Linseeds are popular in Eastern Europe as a seasoning for soft cream cheese and they are sometimes sprinkled on potatoes. Linseeds are also made into strongly flavoured oil, which needs to be kept in the dark or it deteriorates. The oil is usually sold as a health supplement in capsule form. Linseeds are suitable for sprouting.

FULL OF:
omega-3, manganese, magnesium, phosphorus, fibre and vitamin B1

HEMP SEEDS

These tiny seeds belong to the cannabis family, although they do not have any of the effects of the psychoactive variant. They have long been used in the cuisines of cultures like China, where they are eaten at the cinema in the way popcorn is eaten in other parts of the world. As well as sprinkling them onto bread, the easiest way to eat hemp seeds is whizzed up in a smoothie or added to muesli or granola. The seeds are also made into oil, which has a lovely nutty flavour and makes an interesting change when used in salad dressings – add a tablespoon to smoothies if you like. The oil is very much worth experimenting with.

FULL OF:
omega-3, -6 and -9, fibre and vitamins B and E

POPPY SEEDS

These tiny seeds come in dark grey and ivory-coloured varieties. They have a distinctive flavour when used in substantial quantities, such as in Eastern European pastries, but are more often used in smaller amounts to give colour and a slight crunch to breads and cakes. They are particularly good added to the batter of citrus cakes and the dark seeds look brilliant in beetroot (beet) cakes. Scatter them over salads that contain brightly coloured ingredients such as carrots or beetroot. They're also lovely tossed with tagliatelle and sprinkled on Italian dumplings, especially those from the north of Italy where gnocchi can be made from bread, beetroot and quark. Poppy seeds are suitable for sprouting.

FULL OF:
fibre, B vitamins, iron, calcium, potassium, manganese, magnesium and zinc

SESAME SEEDS

Sesame seeds come in various colours – brown, red, black, yellow and cream. The darker seeds have more flavour and look great in many dishes. Sesame seeds are prevalent in the cuisines of the Middle East, Greece, Turkey and the Balkans, especially in pastries and bread. They also form the basis of tahini paste, which is used to make nutty dressings, and the chickpea (garbanzo bean) dip, hummus. Sesame seeds are also made into oil, which has a long shelf life and is very stable. The oil is much used in South-East Asia – both in cooking and in dressings – and is valued for its very strong, distinctive flavour. When used for dressings it's best to mix it with a milder oil such as sunflower or peanut. Sesame seeds are suitable for sprouting.

FULL OF:
manganese, calcium, magnesium, iron, phosphorus and vitamin B1

CHIA SEEDS

These seeds have been dubbed the new super food because they contain more omega-3 fatty acids than salmon, plus a wide range of antioxidants and minerals. They have become particularly popular in the US and among athletes, as they are said to build muscle. It is also claimed that they can lower cholesterol and reduce the risk of heart disease. Originally from South America, the flavour of the seeds is pretty mild and this has advantages – you can add them to many of the things you already cook without noticing that they're there. Consider adding them to pilaffs, soups, smoothies, bread, muesli, granola, porridge, cookies and cakes. They are also suitable for sprouting.

FULL OF:
protein, fibre, calcium, iron and B vitamins

WATTLE SEEDS

Aboriginal Australians have long been aware of the unique flavour and nutritional value of wattle seeds, obtained from certain species of the acacia tree. Roasted wattle seeds have been variously described as tasting like coffee, chocolate, hazelnut and freshly baked bread. They can be milled into a highly nutritious flour to make bread, or used to flavour ice creams, mousses and drinks. They are also good as a coating or rub for roast beef, lamb and venison, as their big flavour works well with strong meaty ingredients. Wattle seeds are not cheap, as the process of harvesting, roasting and grinding is very labour intensive. For this reason they have been seen as a gourmet ingredient, although this is changing.

FULL OF:
carbohydrates, fibre and protein. Research into the medicinal properties is ongoing.

PULSES & LEGUMES

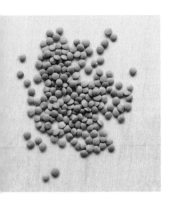

BROWN LENTILS

Brown lentils are sometimes known as continental or Egyptian lentils and come in a range of shades from khaki to dark black. They retain their shape well during cooking although you shouldn't cook them too vigorously or they can easily turn mushy. They are a little bigger than green lentils with a slightly more 'solid' skin, and have a stronger and earthier flavour. They can be cooked in water, drained and then flavoured or tossed with vinaigrette, or cooked in stock that is absorbed as they soften. Some cooks think salting lentils before they are cooked toughens them, but this is subjective. I salt them.

SOAKING & COOKING:

no soaking
cook for 15—40 minutes, depending on age

FULL OF:

fibre, protein, folic acid, manganese, iron, vitamins B1 and B6 and potassium

GREEN LENTILS

Green lentils retain their shape and are a little less mealy than brown lentils. They have a mild, gentle flavour and look prettier than brown lentils. Some cooks think salting lentils before they're cooked toughens them, but this is subjective. I salt them. They can be cooked in water, drained and then flavoured or tossed with vinaigrette, or cooked in stock that is absorbed as they soften.

SOAKING & COOKING:

no soaking
cook for 15—40 minutes, depending on age

FULL OF:

fibre, protein, folic acid, manganese, iron, vitamins B1 and B6 and potassium

PUY LENTILS

French puy lentils are very small blue-green lentils with slight marbling. They stay intact when cooked – unless you boil them fiercely – and have a lovely, peppery flavour. Umbrian lentils, sometimes called Castelluccio lentils, are similarly classy and expensive. Both varieties keep their shape well and make superb salads. Because they are bland but earthy they are brilliant paired with strong flavours like smoked fish, roast capsicums (bell peppers), anchovies and feta. Simmer in water, drain and then flavour or toss with vinaigrette. Alternatively, cook in stock that will be absorbed as they soften. Some cooks think salting lentils before they are cooked toughens them, but I salt them.

SOAKING & COOKING:

no soaking
cook for 20—30 minutes, depending on age

FULL OF:

fibre, protein, folic acid, manganese, iron, vitamins B1 and B6 and potassium

RED LENTILS

Red lentils are tiny, split lentils that collapse into a thick purée when cooked. They make brilliant soups and Indian dal. If an Indian recipe calls for more unusual lentils and I can't find them, I'll use red lentils instead. They seem to go very well with both Indian and Middle Eastern spices and flavourings – and cook incredibly quickly. Red lentils always soften so feel free to salt them before they are cooked. One of my favourite mid-week meals is made from red lentils cooked with chopped tomatoes, capsicums (bell peppers), onions, garlic, cumin and ground coriander. This dish is quite mild and soothing and is great eaten, as dal should be, with hot pickles and chutneys.

SOAKING & COOKING:

no soaking
cook for 15—20 minutes

FULL OF:

fibre, protein, folic acid, manganese, iron, vitamins B1 and B6 and potassium

SPLIT PEAS

Split peas can be yellow (the sweetest) or green and take longer to cook than lentils. They eventually collapse into a chunky, earthy-tasting purée. They always soften so feel free to salt them before they are cooked. Both kinds of split peas are good in soup, especially when made with strongly flavoured stock such as ham. Yellow split peas tend to be used more in Mediterranean soups while green peas are more common in the soups of northern climes. In Greece and Turkey purées of yellow split peas are served as a mezze, thick with olive oil and flavoured with garlic and sometimes herbs and spices.

SOAKING & COOKING:
no soaking
cook for 45–90 minutes, depending on age

FULL OF:
fibre, protein, iron, vitamin B1 and folic acid

HARICOT BEANS

The small white haricot bean becomes meltingly tender when cooked, without falling apart. It is not too starchy and has a nice skin that is not too thick. Haricot beans are used in many classic bean dishes such as baked beans and cassoulet, and are also excellent in salads and stews. In the US they are known as navy beans and are used to make Boston baked beans. Some people believe that salting beans before they are cooked toughens their skins – I agree.

SOAKING & COOKING:
soak dried haricot beans for 4 hours
cook for 1 hour–1 hour 30 minutes, depending on age

FULL OF:
fibre, protein, iron, potassium, selenium, thiamine, vitamin B6 and folic acid

FLAGEOLET BEANS

Small and pale green, flageolets are delicious and more delicate than many other dried beans. They require less cooking than most beans and have a thin skin and a creamy texture. I don't salt them until they are tender as I think it toughens their skins. In French cuisine flageolets are much prized and often eaten with lamb. They can't take big flavours and are best tossed in melted butter, olive oil and herbs, or with cream.

SOAKING & COOKING:
soak dried flageolets for 4 hours
cook for about 1 hour, depending on age

FULL OF:
fibre, protein, potassium and vitamin B9

BORLOTTI BEANS

These Italian beans, known in the US as cranberry beans, are large and plump with a pinkish-brown skin and crimson markings. When cooked they lose their brightness and turn pale brown. They have a distinctive, slightly bitter flavour and a creamy texture, and are used in a wide variety of Italian and Portuguese dishes. Because they hold their shape well they're perfect in the Italian pasta and bean soup *pasta e fagioli*, and bean salads. When cooking, it's best not to salt them until they are tender as it toughens the skin. It's also a good idea to keep a couple of tins of cooked borlotti beans in the cupboard.

SOAKING & COOKING:
soak dried borlotti beans for 4 hours
cook for 1 hour–1 hour 30 minutes, depending on age

FULL OF:
fibre, protein, vitamin B1, iron, potassium, phosphorus, magnesium and folic acid

CHICKPEAS

Chickpeas – known as garbanzo beans in the US – are nutty, firm and golden in colour, and shaped like hazelnuts. I can't detect much difference between home-cooked chickpeas and the tinned variety, so I rarely cook them from scratch. However, the nutritional content of home-cooked chickpeas is slightly higher and they are also cheaper. Chickpeas are widely used in Middle Eastern cooking, where they form the basis of hummus, as well as in India. Don't salt them until they are tender as this can toughen the skins. Chickpeas are hard to cook to tenderness.

SOAKING & COOKING:
soak dried chickpeas overnight
cook for 2 hours 30 minutes–4 hours, depending on age

FULL OF:
manganese, folic acid, iron, molybdenum (a trace mineral that helps the body produce detoxifying enzymes) and phosphorus

PINTO BEANS

Pinto or 'painted' beans are so-called because their orangey-pink skins have russet-coloured streaks. Pintos are the beans originally used in Mexican refried beans and are still popular in South America, although nowadays other varieties of beans are also used. Don't salt them until they are tender as this can toughen the skins.

SOAKING & COOKING:
soak dried pinto beans for 4 hours
cook for 1 hour 30 minutes

FULL OF:
fibre, protein, molybdenum (a trace mineral that helps the body produce detoxifying enzymes), folic acid, manganese, phosphorus, vitamin B1 and magnesium

BLACK BEANS

Also known as turtle beans in the US, black beans are small, black and shiny and have a velvety texture, but still manage to keep their shape when cooked. Don't salt them until they are tender as this can toughen the skins. Black beans are closely related to haricots and some people prefer them in chilli to kidney beans. They are much used in South American and Caribbean cooking – they make a spectacular spicy bean soup – and are the main constituent of the Brazilian national dish, *feijoada*. Black beans are also good for salads and their slightly mushroomy flavour makes them one of the best beans for wintry soups and stews.

SOAKING & COOKING:
soak dried black beans for 4 hours
cook for about 1 hour 30 minutes, depending on age

FULL OF:
fibre, protein, molybdenum (a trace mineral that helps the body produce detoxifying enzymes), folic acid, manganese, magnesium, vitamin B1, phosphorus and iron

ADZUKI BEANS

Small and shiny red, adzuki beans (also known as aduki beans, red chori or red cow peas) are grown and eaten in Japan and China, most commonly used in sweet dishes and as bean paste. They are also cooked with rice – turning the grain a pale pink colour in a classic Japanese dish called red-cooked festival rice – and are very good in salads. They can also be added to soups. Don't salt them until they are tender as this can toughen the skins.

SOAKING & COOKING:
soak dried adzuki beans for 4 hours
cook for 1 hour–1 hour 30 minutes, depending on age

FULL OF:
fibre, protein, magnesium, potassium, iron, zinc, manganese and B vitamins

CANNELLINI BEANS

Cannellini beans are similar to haricots but a bit bigger and have a fluffier texture. They are related to French soissons beans and are much loved by Italians, especially in Tuscany. Cannellini beans are a very good all-purpose bean, and are not too expensive. I don't salt them before they are tender as I think this toughens their skins. Tinned cannellini beans are a brilliant store cupboard standby for making salads or adding to soups. Heat them with fried onions, garlic and a little chicken stock and purée them for a delicious side dish – make sure you add plenty of seasoning and a generous slug of olive oil. They are the best bean for the classic Italian bean and tuna salad, *tonno e fagioli*.

SOAKING & COOKING:
soak dried cannellini beans for 4 hours
cook for about 2 hours. depending on age

FULL OF:
fibre. iron, magnesium, folic acid and vitamin B1

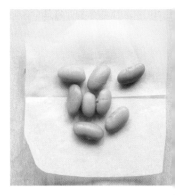

BUTTERBEANS

Butterbeans are big, starchy and thick-skinned with a flavour similar to potato. Some people have bad memories of being served butterbeans at school, which is perhaps why they are not more popular. They are good with assertive ingredients such as mustard and chorizo, in meaty stews and as a side dish with pork. Good seasoning and a handful of herbs tossed through improves them considerably. They are also very good when tossed with cooked spinach. Spaniards use them to make a great rib-sticking stew with onions, tomatoes, paprika and black pudding. Some people believe that salting beans before they are cooked toughens their skins and I agree.

SOAKING & COOKING:
soak dried butterbeans for 4 hours
cook for 1 hour–1 hour 30 minutes. depending on age

FULL OF:
fibre. protein, folic acid, manganese, magnesium and potassium

BLACK-EYED PEAS

Black-eyed peas – also known as black-eyed beans – are small, creamy beans with a distinctive black stripe where they were joined to the pod. They keep their shape well during cooking, making them a good salad ingredient. They are very popular in dishes of the American South, Africa and the Caribbean, where they are frequently combined with rice. It's best not to salt them until they are tender as this can toughen the skins.

SOAKING & COOKING:
soak dried black-eyed peas for 4 hours
cook for 1 hour–1 hour 30 minutes. depending on age

FULL OF:
fibre, protein, potassium, iron, folic acid, zinc and magnesium

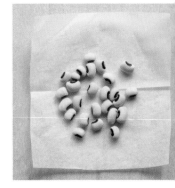

KIDNEY BEANS

Kidney beans are quite large compared to other beans, reddish-brown in colour and thick-skinned; they retain their shape well even after long cooking. Kidney beans can stand up to big spicy flavours, which is why they are widely used in dishes such as chilli con carne, Mexican soups and Caribbean food. Other beans will be discoloured if they are cooked in the same pan, as kidney beans turn the water dark reddish-pink. Don't salt them until they are tender as this toughens the skins. Dried kidney beans need soaking and careful cooking as their outer skins contain toxins when raw, but rinsing and boiling eliminates this.

SOAKING & COOKING:
soak dried kidney beans for 4 hours, boil for 15 minutes in fresh water. drain, rinse and cook in more fresh water for 1 hour 30 minutes—2 hours, depending on age

FULL OF:
fibre. protein, molybdenum (a trace mineral that helps the body produce detoxifying enzymes). iron, folic acid, magnesium. manganese and vitamin B1

MUNG BEANS

Mung beans can be bought whole or split and are one of the smallest beans. They are a lovely olive colour and have quite a fresh taste for a dried bean. They are used a lot in Indian and South-East Asian cooking, mainly in stews and soups. Don't salt them until they are tender as this can toughen the skins.

SOAKING & COOKING:
soak dried mung beans for 4 hours
cook for about 1 hour, depending on age

FULL OF:
fibre, protein, folic acid, iron, zinc, potassium, magnesium, manganese, phosphorus and vitamin B1

BROAD BEANS

Fresh, sweet broad (fava) beans are only available for a short time and are at their best in early summer. Frozen broad beans are available but their flavour is not as good. Very young broad beans can be eaten straight from the pod – Italians eat them with prosciutto and shaved pecorino. Unless the beans are very young and tender it is best to slip off their skins after cooking. They work well in a wide variety of dishes, from pasta to pilaffs. In Sicily and the Middle East, purées made from dried broad beans, olive oil and garlic are common. Dried broad beans are also the main ingredient for the Middle Eastern fritters known as falafel. When cooking dried broad beans don't salt them until they are tender as this can toughen the skins.

SOAKING & COOKING:
soak dried broad beans for 4 hours
cook for about 2 hours, depending on age

FULL OF:
fibre, iron, phosphorus, potassium, vitamins A and B1

SOYA BEANS

There are over 1000 varieties of these ancient beans, which come in a wide variety of sizes and colours including white, yellow, green, brown and black. They are extremely nutritious and widely used in Chinese and Japanese cooking in a variety of forms, from sauces to sprouts. Dried soya beans are soaked, boiled and used in soups, stews and salads. Edamame are immature soya beans usually served and eaten in the pod, and in Japan they are popular sprinkled with salt. Edamame make a lovely salad ingredient – fresh and green – and are very easy to digest.

SOAKING & COOKING:
soak dried soya beans overnight
cook for about 3 hours, depending on age

FULL OF:
fibre, protein, calcium, folic acid, iron, magnesium, manganese, potassium, phosphorus, zinc, B vitamins and vitamins C and K

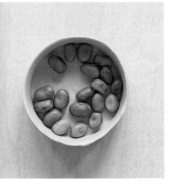

FUL MEDAMES

These small brown beans – shaped like little broad beans – are mostly used in Egypt for what is considered their national dish. The beans are simply soaked, cooked, doused in olive oil and flavoured with cumin and raw onion. It's usual to eat this with hard-boiled eggs and is often served for breakfast. The beans have a lovely nutty flavour but they do require very long, slow cooking. Don't salt them until they are tender as it can toughen the skins. It isn't as easy to find ful medames as the other beans listed here – look for them in Middle Eastern stores.

SOAKING & COOKING:
soak dried ful medames overnight
cook for 2–4 hours, depending on age

FULL OF:
fibre, protein, copper, iron, folic acid, magnesium, manganese, zinc, calcium and phosphorus, plus vitamins A, B6 and C

WHOLEGRAIN RICE

Wholegrain rice comes in different lengths of grain – long, medium and short – and in several colours. The flavour is slightly nutty and the texture is chewy compared to white rice. Wholegrain rice takes longer to cook and doesn't absorb liquid in the same way white rice does, which makes it a troublesome substitute for some classic rice dishes. However, like many whole grains, it makes a great salad base because the grains stay firm and separate. It can be cooked in lightly salted water and drained, or in stock, allowing the stock to become absorbed as the grain softens.

SOAKING & COOKING:

no soaking
cooks in 40—50 minutes, less if pre-soaked in water

FULL OF:

vitamins B1, B3 and B6, phosphorus, iron, manganese, magnesium and selenium

BROWN RISOTTO RICE

Risotto made with brown risotto rice is slightly different in texture from the creamy risotto made with its white rice counterpart. Brown risotto rice takes longer to cook and this problem is exacerbated when you need to simmer (rather than boil) the grains, as you do with risotto. One way around this is to cook brown rice risotto long and slow in the oven, stirring briefly only at the beginning and the end. This produces delicious results when teamed with ingredients such as pumpkin (winter squash), mushrooms, bacon and chestnuts. It is also a good alternative to wholegrain paella rice, which can be expensive and difficult to find.

SOAKING & COOKING:

no soaking
cooks in 50—60 minutes

FULL OF:

vitamins B1, B3 and B6, phosphorus, iron, manganese, magnesium and selenium

BROWN SHORT-GRAIN RICE

This is a wholegrain version of pudding rice but it is very difficult to make a rice pudding with this grain alone, as it doesn't become creamy enough. However, used in conjunction with white pudding rice it makes a lovely and creamy pudding that is slightly chewy with a good nutty flavour. This rice pudding is excellent with dried fruit compotes and makes a good breakfast if you don't like, or want a change from, porridge. You can cook the grains in milk and water, or use coconut milk and vary the flavourings. In India a rice pudding is made with crushed cardamom and grated apple, which cooks along with the rice.

SOAKING & COOKING:

no soaking
cooks in 40—50 minutes

FULL OF:

vitamins B1, B3 and B6, phosphorus, iron, manganese, magnesium and selenium

CAMARGUE RED RICE

This is one of the coloured rices that are becoming increasingly popular along with black rice from Italy and another red rice produced in Bhutan. These rices are valued as much for their lovely taste as how good they look on the plate. Camargue red rice is cultivated in the wetlands of the Camargue region of south-west France and is readily available in the UK. Like brown wholegrain rice it has a chewy texture, although it does become softer than brown rice when cooked. You can cook it in plain water and drain it, or simmer it in stock, allowing the stock to become absorbed as the grain softens.

SOAKING & COOKING:

no soaking
cooks in 35—45 minutes

FULL OF:

B vitamins, iron, calcium and the antioxidant anthocyanin

WHEAT

The high gluten content of wheat-based flour makes it ideal for making bread. As well as plain (all-purpose) white flour, self-raising wholemeal (whole-wheat), plain wholemeal and strong wholemeal flours are available. The latter is perfect for bread while the others are used for pastry and cakes. Some white flour is often used with wholemeal when making sweet baked goods to give a softer, less dense result. Wholemeal flour is more nutritious than white and can actually improve the flavour of some dishes where white is traditionally used. Wheat grain is less widely available in Europe than in the US, where it is called wheat berry, but can be sourced online or in speciality shops. Both soft and hard (more chewy) varieties are available.

SOAKING & COOKING:
soak wheat grain overnight
cook soft wheat grain for 40 minutes; cook hard wheat grain for 1–2 hours

FULL OF:
fibre, protein, iron, calcium, potassium and vitamins B and E

SPELT

Spelt is an ancient wheat now available as white and wholemeal (whole-wheat) flour, as well as grain. It is more readily available than it once was and can be eaten by some people who are intolerant to regular wheat, although it still contains gluten. Spelt grain becomes quite creamy when stirred so it can be used to make risotto in the same way that pearl barley can, although it isn't quite as starchy. Spelt and farro can be interchanged in cooking but they do have different properties. Pearled (all bran removed) and semi-pearled (some bran left on) are both available, although pearled is easier to find. Cook in water and drain, or in stock by the absorption method.

SOAKING & COOKING:
no soaking
cooks in about 45 minutes

FULL OF:
fibre, protein, B vitamins, zinc and manganese

FARRO

Farro is an ancient wheat that can be used in soups, stews and salads. It can also be used in risottos as it becomes slightly creamy when simmered in stock and stirred, although never as creamy as pearl barley or spelt. As a salad base it is delicious dressed with vinaigrette and works well with a range of flavours, from Scandinavian hot smoked salmon and dill, to Middle Eastern pomegranates and coriander (cilantro). Farro is most commonly sold semi-pearled (labelled *semi-perlato*) and is the version used in this book. Like freekeh, spelt and wheat, farro softens when cooked but remains a little firm.

SOAKING & COOKING:
no soaking for semi-pearled farro; soak non-pearled farro overnight
cook semi-pearled farro for 20–40 minutes; cook non-pearled farro for 60–70 minutes

FULL OF:
protein, fibre, iron, niacin, zinc and magnesium

FREEKEH

Freekeh is roasted green wheat with a strong smoky taste, which is widely used in Syria, Lebanon and Egypt. It stands up well to big flavours – preserved lemon, dried fruit and pomegranate molasses for example – and is great with barbecued food. Freekeh does not need soaking and cooks in 30 minutes; boil in water and drain, or cook in stock by the absorption method. It can be used instead of burghul (bulgur wheat) for the pilaffs in the book – just increase the cooking time – to produce a less fluffy, slightly chewier and wonderfully substantial dish.

SOAKING & COOKING:
no soaking
cooks in 30 minutes

FULL OF:
fibre, protein, calcium and iron

WILD RICE

This is not technically rice but the grain from a water grass native to North America. It is, however, cooked and eaten like rice. Wild rice never softens but retains a chewy texture and a pronounced nutty flavour and is best eaten with other rices such as Camargue red or brown rice. The long black grains contrast well with brightly coloured ingredients such as corn and roast capsicums (bell peppers). Cook in stock until the stock has reduced, or boil in water, drain and toss with melted butter or oil and seasonings. If eaten cold, toss with dressing while still warm.

SOAKING & COOKING:
no soaking
cooks in 35—50 minutes

FULL OF:
fibre, folic acid, zinc, magnesium, phosphorus, manganese and vitamin B6

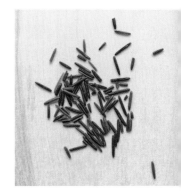

CORN

Corn, also known as maize, is a native American grass. It comes in many colours ranging from blue-grey to yellow and has a characteristic sweet flavour. It's eaten in many forms, including barbecued corn on the cob, Italian polenta and 'grits'. When buying polenta look for the coarsely ground variety that looks like bright yellow couscous. It needs long and slow cooking with water or stock, which is absorbed to produce a kind of smooth porridge. Butter and cheese are often added, or cooked polenta can be spread out, left to set and then cut into shapes and fried. Coarse or medium-ground corn can be added to cakes or cookies to give a sweet corn taste and a slightly gritty texture.

SOAKING & COOKING:
no soaking
cooks in 1—2 hours. For quick-cook polenta follow packet instructions.

FULL OF:
fibre, protein, vitamins B, C and E, phosphorus and magnesium

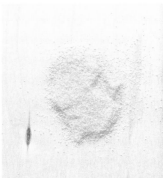

BARLEY

Pearl (or pearled) barley is processed barley that has had the germ and some bran removed from the grain. While not strictly a whole grain, pearl barley is used in this book for two reasons: it is the version most readily available in the shops and, unlike most grains, barley's fibre is not concentrated in its outer bran but found right through the kernel. This means that pearl barley contains at least 8% fibre and retains much of the distinctive earthy flavour of unprocessed barley. Feel free to use unprocessed barley (often referred to as pot barley or Scotch barley) instead – just follow the soaking and cooking instructions provided here and continue the recipe as for pearl barley.

SOAKING & COOKING:
soak pot or Scotch barley overnight; no soaking for pearl barley
cook pot or Scotch barley for 40—50 minutes; cook pearl barley for about 30 minutes

FULL OF:
fibre, phosphorus and manganese

QUINOA

Quinoa is a versatile South American grain-like crop that can be eaten hot or cold, and is similar to couscous and burghul (bulgur wheat) in texture and size. Quinoa benefits from being toasted in a dry frying pan for a minute before cooking in liquid for 10–15 minutes. The cooking instructions on most brands suggest using more liquid than necessary; 675 ml (23 fl oz) per 300 g (10½ oz/1½ cups) quinoa is enough to produce a moist grain that fluffs up well like couscous. Quinoa is a gluten-free complete protein (rare in the plant world), which means it contains all the amino acids we need. Quinoa is available in white, black and red versions, flakes (that can be treated like oat flakes) and flour.

SOAKING & COOKING:
no soaking
cooks in 10—15 minutes

FULL OF:
iron and calcium, and also a good source of manganese, magnesium and fibre

RYE

Rye is a cold-weather grain that can be grown in chilly and wet northern climates, which is why so many breads from Northern and Eastern Europe are made with rye flour. Its low gluten content produces a dense loaf and for this reason it is often combined with wheat flour. Rye kernels are less common than rye flour, but still make good eating with their heavy, slightly sweet and almost fruity flavour. They are excellent added to soups and stews, especially those made with ingredients such as venison, beetroot (beet), smoked meat or red cabbage. Rye kernels also make a great salad base and team well with dill, caraway, plain or smoked salmon, red berries, yoghurt and buttermilk.

SOAKING & COOKING:
soak rye grain overnight
cooks in 60—70 minutes

FULL OF:
fibre, protein, manganese, phosphorus, zinc, potassium, iron, calcium, magnesium, vitamin E and various B vitamins

BUCKWHEAT

Buckwheat is technically a leafy seed grain and has been a staple for centuries in Russia and Eastern Europe. Buckwheat groats and roasted buckwheat (known as kasha) both have an assertive 'meaty' flavour, particularly the roasted variety. Unroasted groats are more palatable and the version to look out for – just quickly toast the groats in a hot pan with a little oil for a minute before cooking in water or stock. Like other grains, buckwheat groats make a good side dish or salad base. For a substantial stuffing for duck or goose try cooked buckwheat groats with prunes, bacon and chestnuts. Buckwheat flour, commonly used in blini, has a gorgeously earthy flavour and is also used in cake batters, pasta and Japanese noodles.

SOAKING & COOKING:
no soaking
cooks in 10—15 minutes

FULL OF:
fibre, manganese and magnesium

AMARANTH

Golden amaranth seeds are considered super grains as they contain all the essential amino acids that make up a perfect protein. They come from a tall leafy plant (the leaves are eaten in many parts of the world) and have an earthy, grassy flavour. They are best popped like corn rather than cooked in liquid – where they quickly disintegrate if overcooked and can be sticky and gruel-like. Pop the seeds and add to breakfast cereals or health bars, but only pop 1 tablespoon at a time because the seeds are so tiny. They can also be added to biscuits (cookies). Amaranth flour is also available – you can use it for flatbreads and cakes – but most people find it produces rather dense baked goods.

SOAKING & COOKING:
no soaking
pops in a few minutes

FULL OF:
protein, calcium, fibre and vitamin E

MILLET

Millet is an ancient grain – probably one of the oldest staple foods – that grows well even in drought-afflicted areas. It is small, mild-tasting and can be interchanged with couscous as it also fluffs up well. Despite its image as a bird food, millet is a good introduction to grains, especially if you are cautious of those with fuller flavours. Nutritionally it is superior to wholegrain rice or wheat and it is gluten-free.

SOAKING & COOKING:
no soaking
cooks in 15—20 minutes

FULL OF:
B vitamins, iron, magnesium, manganese, phosphorus and zinc

KAMUT

Technically called khorasan but commonly sold under the brand name Kamut, this is an ancient variety of wheat related to durum. It has large honey-coloured kernels that make an excellent base for salads. Kamut contains 20–40 per cent more protein than conventional wheat and has a less wheaty taste; it is good paired with assertive flavours such as preserved lemon, capers, anchovies and feta. Once cooked, it keeps well in the refrigerator for a couple of days and is also available in flour form.

SOAKING & COOKING:
soak overnight
cooks in 50—60 minutes

FULL OF:
protein, fibre, iron, zinc, vitamins B2, B3 and E, phosphorus and magnesium

BURGHUL

Burghul, or bulgur wheat, much used in Turkish, Greek and Middle Eastern cooking, is one of the quickest and easiest starches to prepare. It is produced when wheat (usually durum) is boiled and then dried, cracked and sorted by size. Burghul is not strictly a whole grain as the outer layers of bran are removed, but still contains plenty of fibre. Cook in boiling water or stock – the time will depend on the coarseness of the grain, so check after 10 minutes. The recipes in this book have been tested with medium burghul. Alternatively, soak in water and eat cold. Do not confuse with cracked wheat, which has not been precooked.

SOAKING & COOKING:
soak for 20 minutes instead of cooking, or cook for 10—15 minutes

FULL OF:
protein, fibre, iron, potassium, phosphorus, manganese and B vitamins

COUSCOUS

Couscous is not actually a grain but a tiny grain-like pellet made from flour and water, traditionally rolled by hand but now commonly produced in factories. Wholemeal (whole-wheat) couscous (made from wholemeal wheat or barley flour) is widely available and has greater health benefits than 'regular' couscous, although it is similar in appearance and flavour. Almost all couscous is precooked. To prepare, pour 3 parts boiling water or stock over 2 parts couscous, cover with plastic wrap and leave for 10–15 minutes. Spices, herbs, nuts, chopped dried fruit or sautéed onions, olive oil or melted butter can be added for flavour. Served cold, couscous makes a good salad; just add vinaigrette and fork through. Giant or Israeli couscous is also available.

SOAKING & COOKING:
soak for 10—15 minutes in boiling water or stock instead of cooking

FULL OF:
fibre and iron (wholemeal/whole-wheat version)

OATS

Freshly harvested oats contain about 14% moisture and must be dried and lightly toasted before the outer casing is removed by grinding. Passing oats through steel cutters produces pinhead and steel cut oats. Rolled (porridge) oats are whole (jumbo) or split grains that have been steamed and flattened to make oat flakes. These make quick porridge and are perfect for muesli and granola. Oatmeal is made from oats ground to various grades; coarse oatmeal is used for porridge while finer oatmeal is used in cookies and bread. Oats can also be used for stuffing, coatings for fish and fish cakes, and can be added to pancakes, muffins, cakes and crumbles. No soaking is necessary before cooking but some people believe it produces a better result.

SOAKING & COOKING:
no soaking
cook oat groats for 60—75 minutes; coarse/steel cut oats for 45 minutes; medium oatmeal 30 minutes; rolled (porridge) oats 6 minutes, jumbo oats 8 minutes

FULL OF:
protein, folic acid, iron, magnesium, calcium, B vitamins and vitamin E

breakfast

SIX GRAIN PORRIDGE

This porridge contains every grain you could possibly want in one bowl, and all are available in flake form. Just buy them individually, combine them yourself and keep the mix to hand so it's always ready to go.

FROM THE GROCER

30 g (1 oz) rye flakes

30 g (1 oz) spelt flakes

20 g (¾ oz) wheat flakes

20 g (¾ oz) barley flakes

20 g (¾ oz) brown rice flakes

20 g (¾ oz) medium oatmeal

20 g (¾ oz) pinhead oatmeal

1.2 litres (41 fl oz) milk or water, or a mixture of both

soft light brown sugar, to taste

full-cream (whole) or low-fat milk (optional)

60 g (2 oz/ ¼) Greek-style yoghurt

60 ml (2 fl oz/¼ cup) runny honey

50 g (1¾ oz) chopped, unsalted pistachio nuts

1 tablespoon sunflower kernels

1 tablespoon chia seeds

1 tablespoon white sesame seeds

FROM THE GREENGROCER

125 g (4½ oz) blueberries

Mix all the flakes and oatmeal together and toast in a dry frying pan over a medium heat for 1 minute. Tip into a saucepan and add the milk or water (or a mixture of both). Bring to the boil then reduce the heat and simmer, stirring from time to time, until thick and soft, about 20 minutes. Add sugar to taste. Divide between four bowls and add a drizzle of milk (if using). Top with the yoghurt, honey, blueberries, pistachio nuts, sunflower kernels, chia seeds and sesame seeds.

COCONUT PORRIDGE
WITH FRESH MANGO & PASSIONFRUIT

This is full of supercharged energy to start the day, and is a little luxurious too. It's great for a weekend brunch.

FROM THE GROCER

400 ml (13½ fl oz) full-cream (whole) milk, plus extra to taste

1 x 400 ml (13½ fl oz) tin coconut milk

75 ml (2½ fl oz) thick (double/heavy) cream, plus extra to taste

50–75 g (1¾–2¾ oz) caster (superfine) sugar, or to taste

175 g (6 oz/1¾ cups) rolled (porridge) oats

FROM THE GREENGROCER

1 mango

2 passionfruit

juice of 2 limes

finely grated zest of 1 lime, plus extra for sprinkling (optional)

Peel the mango and slice the cheeks from each side of the stone, keeping as close to the stone as possible. Neatly cut the cheeks into pieces about 3 mm (⅛ in) thick. Halve the passionfruit; scoop out the pulp and seeds and mix with the mango and half the lime juice. Set aside while you make the porridge but don't prepare the fruit too far in advance or it will go soft.

Put the milk, coconut milk, cream, 50 g (1¾ oz) of the sugar and the oats into a saucepan. Add the lime zest and bring to just under a boil – you must not boil the coconut milk, so make sure it is just gently simmering. Simmer for 5 minutes, stirring a little, until the mixture is thick – if it is getting too thick for your liking then add a little more milk. Once cooked add the remaining lime juice and more milk or cream to get the consistency you want. Taste for sugar and adjust that too if desired.

Pour the porridge into serving bowls and sprinkle with extra lime zest (if using). Top with the mango and passionfruit, or serve them on the side.

WARM MUESLI
WITH COOKED APPLES & MAPLE SYRUP

You can double or triple the quantities for the muesli and store it in an airtight container for up to two weeks. The muesli can be eaten plain with cold milk or heated and served warm with apple as described below.

FROM THE GROCER

175 g (6 oz/1¾ cups) rolled (porridge) oats with wheat bran, or standard rolled oats

25 g (1 oz) pistachio nuts, chopped

50 g (1¾ oz) hazelnuts, chopped

50 g (1¾ oz) pitted dates, chopped

50 g (1¾ oz) dried cranberries

2 tablespoons raisins

20 g (¾ oz) white sesame seeds

50 g (1¾ oz) sunflower kernels

10 g (¼ oz) hemp seeds

10 g (¼ oz) linseeds (flax seeds)

100 ml (3½ fl oz) milk per person, to serve

10 g (¼ oz) unsalted butter per person, to serve

1 teaspoon golden caster (superfine) sugar per person, to serve

Greek-style yoghurt, to serve

maple syrup, to serve

FROM THE GREENGROCER

½ cored apple per person, to serve

For the muesli, mix together the oats, pistachio nuts, hazelnuts, dates, cranberries, raisins, sesame seeds, sunflower kernels, hemp seeds and linseeds. You can store this mixture in an airtight container for up to 2 weeks.

To cook the muesli, put 100 g (3½ oz) muesli mix and 100 ml (3½ fl oz) milk per person into a saucepan. Heat until almost boiling; stir gently, then remove from the heat and leave to stand for 5 minutes, covered, so that the oats can soften.

Cut the ½ apple per person into thin wedges about 5 mm (¼ in) thick. Melt the butter in a non-stick frying pan over a medium heat and sauté the apple on both sides until golden and tender on the outside – the pieces can still be a little firm in the middle. Sprinkle with the sugar and toss to caramelise for 30–45 seconds.

Serve the warm muesli with the yoghurt and the apples spooned on top, drizzled with a little maple syrup.

HOME-MADE GRANOLA
AMERICAN STYLE

This is so much more delicious than anything you can buy and once you've made it you will never go back to commercial stuff. Add your own fresh fruit to it as well – banana, plum, apple or pear – and yoghurt too.

FROM THE GROCER

400 g (14 oz/4 cups) rolled (porridge) oats

75 g (2¾ oz) chopped pecans

35 g (1¼ oz) roughly chopped hazelnuts

60 g (2 oz/½ cup) sunflower kernels

60 g (2 oz) pumpkin seeds (pepitas)

60 g (2 oz) linseeds (flax seeds)

60 g (2 oz) hemp seeds

250 ml (8½ fl oz/1 cup) maple syrup

60 g (2 oz/⅓ cup, lightly packed) soft light brown sugar

80 ml (2½ fl oz/⅓ cup) rapeseed, peanut or hazelnut oil

150 g (5½ oz/2 cups) dried apples, chopped

75 g (2¾ oz) dried cranberries

35 g (1¼ oz) raisins

Preheat the oven to 160°C (320°F). Line one large or two small roasting tins with baking paper.

Put the oats and all the nuts and seeds into a bowl and mix them together. Put the maple syrup, sugar and oil into a large heavy-based saucepan over a low heat, stirring a little to help the sugar melt. Stir in the oats, nuts and seeds and mix well until all the dry ingredients are coated. Spread the mixture over the lined trays – break it up a bit as it shouldn't lie in big clumps – and bake for about 25 minutes, or until golden. Stir through the dried fruit and cook for another 5 minutes. Remove from the oven and leave to set and cool. Break the granola into chunks and store in an airtight container.

If you want to have it warm for breakfast you can just reheat it in the oven – this will crisp and refresh it too – or eat it with warm milk. The granola will keep well for 2 weeks and you can refresh it by putting it all in the oven again for 15 minutes or so.

QUICK IDEAS
breakfast

Polenta porridge with grapes & seeds

Put 50 g (1¾ oz/⅓ cup) polenta and 1 tablespoon sugar into a saucepan and mix in 300 ml (10 fl oz) boiling water and 150 ml (5 fl oz) hot milk, stirring. Cook over a gentle heat for 30 minutes (or 15 minutes for quick-cook polenta), stirring. Add more hot water if needed. Sauté 60 g (2 oz) seedless red grapes in a knob of butter until soft, adding a splash of saba or grape juice towards the end. Top the polenta with the buttery grapes and toasted sunflower kernels. Serves 2.

Farro porridge with yoghurt & apricots

Cook 50 g (1¾ oz) semi-pearled farro in water until tender. Drain and place in a saucepan with 175 ml (6 fl oz) milk and 2 teaspoons light brown sugar. Simmer for 15 minutes, stirring from time to time. Place in a bowl and top with some Greek-style yoghurt, 35 g (1¼ oz) dried apricots that have been simmered in apple juice and roughly chopped, and 1 teaspoon each chopped pistachio nuts, sunflower kernels, pumpkin seeds (pepitas) and chia seeds. Serves 1.

Proper Scottish porridge with stewed apples, honey & linseeds

Stew 1 chopped bramley apple with 2 tablespoons water until soft. Put 25 g (1 oz) each of medium and pinhead oatmeal into a saucepan and toast for 3 minutes. Slowly add 300 ml (10 fl oz) water and cook gently, stirring a little, for 25 minutes. Stir in some milk. Add 1 tablespoon heather honey to the apple and serve with the porridge. Sprinkle with toasted linseeds (flax seeds). Serves 1.

Quinoa porridge with pink grapefruit, pumpkin seeds & chia seeds

Simmer 50 g (1¾ oz/¼ cup) quinoa in 250 ml (8½ fl oz/1 cup) water for 15 minutes. The water should become absorbed. Add 100 ml (3½ fl oz) milk, 2 tablespoons thick (double/heavy) cream, some freshly grated nutmeg, a pinch of ground cinnamon,1 tablespoon chia seeds and 2 teaspoons sugar. Simmer for 5 minutes until you have a thick soupy mixture. Top with the segments of ½ ruby grapefruit and some pumpkin seeds (pepitas). Serves 1.

Super bowl muesli

Combine 25 g (1 oz) each of malted wheat flakes, crisp spelt flakes, rye flakes, quinoa flakes, rolled (porridge) oats, barley flakes, brown rice flakes, popped amaranth and goji berries; 50 g (1¾ oz) each of dried cherries, cranberries, toasted and chopped hazelnuts; 1 tablespoon each chia and hemp seeds, linseeds (flax seeds), sunflower kernels, pumpkin seeds (pepitas), wheatgerm and wheat bran. Makes 400 g (14 oz). Serve 1 portion (50 g/1¾ oz) with 100 ml (3½ fl oz) milk. Keep in an airtight container.

Honey-puffed wholegrain cereal

Gently heat 300 g (10½ oz) honey and 60 ml (2 fl oz/¼ cup) sunflower oil in a large saucepan. Stir in 200 g (7 oz) mixed puffed grains (wheat, oats, rice, spelt and amaranth), 50 g (1¾ oz) each chopped pecans, hazelnuts, sunflower kernels, pumpkin seeds (pepitas), linseeds (flax seeds) and hemp seeds and 2 tablespoons chia seeds. Spread over 2 lined baking trays and bake for 35–40 minutes at 160°C (320°F), but check how it's going after 20 minutes. Leave to cool and then break up any clumps. Makes 600 g (1 lb 5 oz).

BUCKWHEAT BLINI
WITH YOGHURT & SMOKED SALMON

These are superb for a weekend brunch party. You can extend the dish by providing finely chopped red onion and small bowls of keta or caviar. Topping the blini with yoghurt is the healthy option but you can of course serve them with crème fraîche or sour cream instead.

FROM THE GROCER

225 g (8 oz) buckwheat or wholemeal (whole-wheat) flour

225 g (8 oz/1½ cups) plain (all-purpose) flour

1½ teaspoons salt

25 g (1 oz) dried active yeast

2 teaspoons caster (superfine) sugar

725 ml (24½ fl oz) warm milk

3 eggs

70 g (2½ oz) butter, melted and cooled

about 125 g (4½ oz) lard, for frying

Greek-style yoghurt, to serve

freshly ground black pepper

FROM THE GREENGROCER

fresh dill sprigs, to serve

lemon wedges, to serve

FROM THE FISHMONGER

smoked salmon slices

Sift the flours into a bowl and add in the bran left behind in the sieve. Mix in the salt. Put the yeast into a cup with 1 teaspoon of the sugar and add about 35 ml (1¼ fl oz) of the warm milk. Stir and set aside somewhere warm for 15 minutes, by which time the yeast should have frothed.

Separate one of the eggs and reserve the egg white. Mix together the yolk and the remaining 2 whole eggs. Make a hollow in the centre of the flour and add the mixed eggs followed by the yeasty milk, the remaining milk and 20 g (¾ oz) of the melted butter. Mix to a smooth batter by gradually whisking the dry ingredients into the wet ones. Cover with a clean tea towel (dish towel) and set aside somewhere warm for 1 hour. Whisk the reserved egg white until stiff but not dry, then fold into the batter.

Melt a little of the lard in a non-stick frying pan over a medium heat. When the lard is hot, spoon in enough batter to make a blinis the size of a saucer. When little bubbles form on the top of the blinis carefully turn it over and cook the other side. Both sides should be light brown and the blinis should be cooked through to the middle. Repeat until all the batter has been used. Place them in a 150°C (300°F) oven as you cook them until ready to serve, separating each with baking paper.

Serve 2 or 3 blini per person. Brush or drizzle them with the remaining melted butter and top with a dollop of Greek-style yoghurt, smoked salmon slices and sprigs of dill. Grind black pepper over the top and offer wedges of lemon alongside.

BUCKWHEAT GALETTES
WITH BACON, EGG, ONIONS & GRUYÈRE

These take a bit of work – they're not difficult, you just need to juggle the components at the end – so they're best served at a casual brunch, lunch or supper. You can omit the fried eggs if you think they are too much.

FROM THE GROCER
125 g (4½ oz) plain (all-purpose) flour
125 g (4½ oz) buckwheat flour
1 teaspoon salt
300 ml (10 fl oz) milk
2 large eggs
30 g (1 oz) butter, melted
75 g (2¾ oz) unsalted butter
salt and freshly ground black pepper
peanut oil, for frying
6 small eggs
150 g (5½ oz) grated gruyère

FROM THE GREENGROCER
2 large onions, very thinly sliced
1 heaped teaspoon chopped
flat-leaf (Italian) parsley

FROM THE BUTCHER
400 g (14 oz) unsmoked lardons

Sift the flours and the 1 teaspoon salt into a bowl and make a well in the centre. In a pitcher, beat together the milk, 125 ml (4 fl oz/½ cup) water and the eggs. Gradually pour this into the well, whisking in the flours as you go until completely smooth. Stir in the melted butter and leave to rest for 30 minutes.

Melt the unsalted butter in a saucepan over a low heat and gently sauté the onions until soft. Turn the heat up a little and cook until golden. Season, transfer to a plate and set aside. Fry the lardons in the same pan – no need to add oil, as they will fry in their own fat – until golden. Set aside with the onions and keep warm.

Heat about a teaspoon of peanut oil in a 25 cm (10 in) non-stick frying pan over a medium heat. Add half a ladleful of batter and swirl it around to cover the base – the galette should be only slightly thicker than a crêpe. Cook until brown on the bottom, then flip and cook the other side. Add a little more oil for each galette but avoid using more than necessary. Keep warm in a 150°C (300°F) oven while you quickly fry the eggs in a little oil – you should be able to do this 3 at a time in two large frying pans.

To serve, spread the onions and lardons over the galettes, then scatter over the gruyère. Top with the eggs and sprinkle with the parsley.

MULTIGRAIN APPLE & CRANBERRY WAFFLES

You don't have to stick to these fruits. Use nectarines in the summer – they shouldn't be too ripe or they'll make the batter wet – and raisins or sour cherries for the dried fruit.

FROM THE GROCER

100 g (3½ oz) malted grain bread flour or malthouse bread flour

100 g (3½ oz/⅔ cup) plain (all-purpose) flour

½ teaspoon baking powder

½ teaspoon bicarbonate of soda (baking soda)

130 g (4½ oz) plain yoghurt

2 eggs

100 ml (3½ fl oz) milk

25 g (1 oz) butter, melted and cooled, plus extra for brushing

1 teaspoon natural vanilla extract

30 g (1 oz/¼ cup) dried cranberries

Greek-style yoghurt or crème fraîche, to serve

roughly chopped toasted pecans, to serve

maple syrup, to serve

FROM THE GREENGROCER

1 apple, peeled, cored and diced

Sift the flours, baking powder and bicarbonate of soda together and put the bran collected in the sieve back into the mixture. In a pitcher, whisk together the yoghurt, eggs, milk, butter and vanilla with a fork.

Make a well in the centre of the flours and pour in the egg and milk mixture. Mix together with a fork, beating to get a nice smooth batter. Stir in the apple and cranberries.

Heat a waffle iron. Brush the inside with melted butter and pour some of the waffle mixture into each compartment. If you are using an electric waffle iron, cook according to the manufacturer's instructions. If you are using a waffle iron that goes on the stovetop, cook over a medium heat for 3–4 minutes each side, turning the iron every minute or so.

Serve topped with yoghurt or crème fraîche, toasted pecans and a drizzle of maple syrup.

QUICK IDEAS
smoothies

Big berry smoothie

BLEND:

1 tablespoon hemp seeds

1½ teaspoons chia seeds

1 banana, chopped

125 ml (4 fl oz/½ cup) acai berry juice

125 ml (4 fl oz/½ cup) pomegranate juice

50 g (1¾ oz/⅓ cup) fresh blueberries

50 g (1¾ oz) raspberries

10 g (¼ oz) dried goji berries

Makes 2 servings

Golden summer smoothie

BLEND:

2 fresh apricots

2 peaches

4 dried apricots

1 tablespoon each sunflower kernels, linseeds (flax seeds) and blanched almonds

2 teaspoons honey

1 tablespoon rolled (porridge) oats

45 g (1½ oz) plain or peach yoghurt

250 ml (8½ fl oz/1 cup) apple juice

Makes 2 servings

Super greens smoothie

BLEND:

250 ml (8½ fl oz/1 cup) pumpkin seed (pepita) milk (page 8)

a handful of baby English spinach leaves

1 avocado, flesh removed

1 banana, chopped

2 teaspoons honey

juice of 1 lime

6 basil leaves

1 tablespoon hemp seeds

1½ teaspoons chia seeds

Makes 2 servings

Mango kulfi smoothie

BLEND:

½ mango, flesh removed

125 ml (4 fl oz/½ cup) mango and apple juice

150 ml (5 fl oz) low-fat milk (or pumpkin seed/pepita or sunflower kernel milk, page 8)

45 g (1½ oz) plain yoghurt

1 tablespoon blanched almonds

2 cardamom pods, seeds ground

1½ teaspoons white sesame seeds

1 teaspoon soft light brown sugar

Makes 2 servings

Big breakfast smoothie

BLEND:

1 banana

4 pitted dates

4 dried apricots

4 tablespoons granola

1 tablespoon sunflower kernels

2 teaspoons linseeds (flax seeds)

1 tablespoon white sesame seeds

1 tablespoon wheatgerm

125 ml (4 fl oz/½ cup) orange juice

150 ml (5 fl oz) low-fat milk

1 tablespoon maple syrup

Makes 2 servings

Beetroot & blues

BLEND:

50 g (1¾ oz) cooked beetroot (beet)

150 g (5½ oz) blueberries

½ apple, cored and chopped

225 ml (7½ fl oz) cranberry juice

small chunk fresh ginger, peeled and chopped

60 g (2 oz/¼ cup) plain yoghurt

1½ teaspoons each chia and hemp seeds, linseeds (flax seeds) and sunflower kernels

1 tablespoon honey

Makes 2 servngs

SERVES : 4   PREPARATION : 15 mins   COOKING : 15 mins

OAT, RICOTTA & BERRY PANCAKES
WITH THYME HONEY

These are so light it's hard to believe they contain oats. Change the berries according to what's in season – blackberries and blackcurrants are good too.

FROM THE GROCER

250 g (9 oz/1 cup) fresh ricotta

3 eggs, 1 whole and 2 separated

50 g (1¾ oz/⅓ cup) wholemeal (whole-wheat) flour

50 g (1¾ oz) soft light brown sugar

25 g (1 oz/¼ cup) rolled (porridge) oats

25 g (1 oz) unsalted butter, melted and cooled, plus non-melted butter for frying

icing (confectioners') sugar, sifted, for dusting

thyme honey or any floral honey

FROM THE GREENGROCER

finely grated zest of 1 lemon

125 g (4½ oz) blueberries or raspberries

Drain the ricotta and mash with the 1 whole egg and the 2 yolks. Add the flour, sugar, oats, melted butter and lemon zest. Gently stir in the berries, mixing carefully so they don't break up too much. Beat the 2 egg whites until stiff and then fold them into the mixture.

Melt a knob of butter in a non-stick frying pan over a medium heat and spoon enough of the batter in to make a pancake the size of your palm. If you are using a fairly big pan you should be able to cook about 3 pancakes at the same time.

Cook the pancakes until set underneath and stable enough to turn. Flip the pancakes and cook until golden and set in the middle. The pancakes should take 3–4 minutes on the first side and 2 minutes on the other. As they cook, remove them from the pan and keep warm in a 150°C (300°F) oven in a single layer or between sheets of baking paper. Add more butter to the pan as needed but be careful not to burn it. Serve the pancakes dusted with icing sugar and drizzled with honey.

PLUM, OAT & ALMOND MUFFINS

Make sure to weigh the plums and not just judge by eye – the amount of plum flesh you have has an impact on the batter, as does ripeness. Over-ripe plums will be too soft and produce a soggy muffin.

FROM THE GROCER

115 g (4 oz) butter, melted and slightly cooled, plus extra for greasing

1 large egg, lightly beaten

150 ml (5 fl oz) full-cream (whole) milk

½ teaspoon natural almond extract

115 g (4 oz) self-raising wholemeal (whole-wheat) flour

a pinch of salt

100 g (3½ oz) soft light brown sugar

85 g (3 oz) rolled (porridge) oats, plus 2 tablespoons for sprinkling

25 g (¾ oz/¼ cup) flaked almonds

1 tablespoon caster (superfine) sugar

icing (confectioners') sugar, sifted, for dusting

FROM THE GREENGROCER

340 g (12 oz) just-ripe plums, halved and stoned

finely grated zest of 1 lemon

Preheat the oven to 180°C (350°F). Grease a 12-hole standard muffin tin with butter and line the holes with circles or squares of baking paper that are large enough to cover the bases and sides.

Cut about 24 thin slices of plum – about 3 mm (⅛ in) at the thickest part – and set aside. Two of these will go on top of each muffin. Dice the rest of the plum flesh and set aside.

In a small bowl, beat the egg, melted butter, milk and almond extract together. In a separate bowl, sift the flour and salt – put the bran back in after sifting – and then add the brown sugar, oats and almonds. Stir the egg and milk mixture into the dry ingredients and add the lemon zest and diced plums. Mix until everything just comes together. Spoon into the muffin cases and sprinkle the remaining oats on top. Lay 2 slices of plum on each muffin and sprinkle with the caster sugar. Bake for 25 minutes. If you put a skewer into the middle of a muffin it should come out clean. When done, leave the muffins in the tin for about 5 minutes, then carefully lift them onto a wire rack. Dust with icing sugar and eat warm or at room temperature. These are best eaten on the day they're made.

APPLE, SOUR CREAM & CINNAMON CRUNCH MUFFINS

Apple pie in a muffin: the layer of crunchy sugariness in the middle makes them stand out from other muffins.

FROM THE GROCER

125 g (4½ oz/1¼ cups) pecans, roughly chopped

1½ tablespoons pumpkin seeds (pepitas)

115 g (4 oz/½ cup, firmly packed) soft dark brown sugar

1½ teaspoons ground cinnamon

200 g (7 oz/1⅓ cups) wholemeal (whole-wheat) flour

200 g (7 oz/1⅓ cups) plain (all-purpose) flour

2 teaspoons baking powder

130 g (4½ oz) butter, cut into cubes

150 g (5½ oz) soft light brown sugar

a pinch of salt

300 g (10 oz) sour cream

1 large egg, lightly beaten

25–50 ml (¾–1¾ fl oz) milk

FROM THE GREENGROCER

250 g (9 oz) granny smith or other tart apples, peeled and chopped

Preheat the oven to 180°C (350°F). To make the sweet spice mix, combine the pecans, pumpkin seeds, soft dark brown sugar and half of the cinnamon. Set aside.

In a large bowl, mix both flours with the baking powder. Add 115 g (4 oz) of the butter and rub it into the dry ingredients with your fingertips. Melt the rest of the butter in a frying pan and sauté the apples until just soft. Stir the apples into the flour mixture together with the soft light brown sugar, salt and the remaining cinnamon. Mix the sour cream with the egg and stir into the dry ingredients. Add the milk gradually, using only as much as you need to make a batter with a reluctant dropping consistency. Don't over-mix; stir just long enough to bring the batter together.

Set 14–16 muffin cases into two 12-hole standard muffin tins. Spoon a heaped tablespoon of batter into each case, sprinkle over some sweet spice mix and evenly distribute the rest of the batter between the muffin cases. Sprinkle the rest of the sweet spice mix on top. Bake for 20 minutes – a skewer inserted into the middle of a muffin should come out clean. Leave to rest in the tin for 5 minutes before lifting the muffins out.

These are nice before they are completely cool, but they're good at room temperature too. It's best to eat them on the day they're baked.

BANANA, MANGO & OAT SMOOTHIE

You can change the fruit here – peach, apricot and passionfruit are all good – but keep the
banana for body.

FROM THE GROCER
450 g (1 lb) plain yoghurt
300 ml (10 fl oz) low-fat milk, or half
milk/half fruit juice (mango, apple and
orange juice are all good)
3 tablespoons rolled (porridge) oats
2 tablespoons runny honey

FROM THE GREENGROCER
1 ripe mango
2 ripe bananas
juice of 1 lime

10 ice cubes

Peel the mango and remove all the flesh, cutting it away from around the
stone. Put the flesh into a blender with all the other ingredients. Hold the
blender lid on as tightly as you can and blend on a low–medium speed
at first to prevent the lid from whizzing off. Turn the speed up and blend
until completely smooth. Taste: you may want to add a little more honey
or lime juice. Serve immediately.

soups

SUMMER SOUPE AU PISTOU

You can make a similar soup in the autumn – just change the vegetables to seasonal ones like carrots and pumpkin (winter squash). You could also make an autumnal pistou with parsley and hazelnuts or walnuts.

FROM THE GROCER

2 tablespoons olive oil

1.7 litres (57 fl oz) chicken stock or water

sea salt flakes and freshly ground black pepper

225 g (8 oz) tinned flageolet or haricot (navy) beans, drained

75 g (2¾ oz) pine nuts

125 ml (4 fl oz/½ cup) extra-virgin olive oil

25 g (1 oz) grated gruyère

25 g (1 oz/¼ cup) grated parmesan, plus extra, to serve

FROM THE GREENGROCER

1 leek, white part only, chopped

1 large potato, chopped into 1.5 cm (½ in) cubes

1 celery stalk, finely chopped

2 zucchini (courgettes), chopped

225 g (8 oz) green beans, trimmed and halved

12 cherry tomatoes, quartered

2 bunches of fresh basil

3 garlic cloves

1 tablespoon chopped flat-leaf (Italian) parsley, to serve

Heat the olive oil in a large heavy-based saucepan. Add the leek and cook over a low heat to soften. Add the potato and celery and cover with the stock or water. Season with salt and pepper, bring to a simmer and then cover and cook for 10 minutes. Add the zucchini, green beans, tinned beans and cherry tomatoes and cook for a further 5 minutes, uncovered.

Meanwhile, make the pistou by putting the basil, garlic, pine nuts and some salt and pepper into a food processor. Add the extra-virgin olive oil while the motor is running. Remove to a bowl and stir in the cheeses. Check for seasoning.

Stir the parsley into the soup and serve hot with a generous spoonful of pistou in each bowl and a sprinkling of parmesan on top. This soup is lovely served with country-style bread.

BLACK BEAN SOUP
WITH AVOCADO SALSA

This offers a real taste of Mexico. Black beans are very earthy and can take a strongly flavoured stock such as ham hock – be prepared to add more than specified to get the consistency you want.

FROM THE GROCER

275 g (9½ oz/1¼ cups) dried black (turtle) beans, soaked overnight

60 ml (2 fl oz/¼ cup) olive oil

2 teaspoons cumin seeds

about 1.5 litres (51 fl oz/6 cups) vegetable or chicken stock

salt and freshly ground black pepper

1 teaspoon ground cumin

80 ml (2½ fl oz/⅓ cup) extra-virgin olive oil

Tabasco sauce, to taste

sour cream, to serve

FROM THE GREENGROCER

1 large onion, finely chopped

1 carrot, chopped

1 celery stalk, plus leaves, finely chopped

3 tablespoons chopped coriander (cilantro) leaves, plus stems from 15 g (½ oz) coriander

1 medium red chilli, seeded and chopped

5 garlic cloves

juice of 1 lime

200 g (7 oz) ripe tomatoes, diced

2 avocados, stoned, flesh diced

2 spring onions (scallions), trimmed and finely chopped

To make the soup, drain the beans and rinse. Heat the olive oil in a heavy-based saucepan and cook the onion, carrot, celery, coriander stems and chilli over a medium heat until pale gold. Stir, then add about 80 ml (2½ fl oz/⅓ cup) water and cover. Leave everything to sweat for about 15 minutes – the vegetables should be quite soft by this stage.

Meanwhile, toast the cumin seeds in a small dry frying pan over a medium heat until fragrant, taking care not to burn them. Grind in a mortar, then transfer to the cooked vegetables with 3 of the garlic cloves (chopped). Cook the vegetables for another 2 minutes and then add the beans and stock. Bring to the boil, reduce the heat and simmer for about 1 hour 30 minutes. The beans should be completely tender. Season and leave to cool completely.

Transfer the beans and about 1 litre (34 fl oz/4 cups) of the cooking liquid to a blender or food processor and purée. Add more liquid if necessary to get the consistency you want. Add half the lime juice and check the seasoning as beans always need plenty of salt and pepper.

Mix together the tomatoes, avocados, ground cumin, the remaining 2 garlic cloves (crushed), spring onions, remaining lime juice, most of the chopped coriander and the extra-virgin olive oil. Season well and add enough Tabasco to give the salsa a good kick.

Ladle the soup into serving bowls and spoon over some sour cream followed by some salsa. Alternatively, serve the salsa on the side. Finish with a sprinkling of chopped coriander.

PUMPKIN, WHITE BEAN & KALE SOUP

It's hard to believe you can make something with such depth of flavour in such a short amount of time.

FROM THE GROCER

80 ml (2½ fl oz/⅓ cup) olive oil

60 ml (2 fl oz/¼ cup) tomato passata (puréed tomatoes)

1.2 litres (41 fl oz) flavoursome chicken or vegetable stock

1 x 400 g (14 oz) tin cannellini (lima) beans, drained and rinsed

2 dried bay leaves

salt and freshly ground black pepper

shaved parmesan, to serve

extra-virgin olive oil, for drizzling

FROM THE GREENGROCER

1 large onion, roughly chopped

750 g (1 lb 11 oz) pumpkin (winter squash), peeled, seeded and cut into small chunks

1 celery stalk, diced

1 large carrot, diced

3 garlic cloves, finely chopped

75 g (2¾ oz) kale or savoy cabbage, coarse stalks removed and leaves shredded

Heat the olive oil in a saucepan over a medium heat. Add the onion, pumpkin, celery and carrot and cook for 8 minutes, or until the vegetables have some colour. Add a splash of water, cover the pan and let the vegetables sweat over a very low heat for 10 minutes. Add the garlic and cook for another couple of minutes, then add the tomato passata, stock, beans, bay leaves and seasoning. Simmer for 10 minutes, then add the kale or cabbage and cook for a further 5 minutes. Check the seasoning and serve with the parmesan sprinkled on top and a good drizzle of the extra-virgin olive oil.

CORN, QUINOA & CAPSICUM SOUP
WITH AVOCADO CREAM

As quinoa is a South American grain, it goes very well with Mexican flavours. You can serve this with avocado salsa instead of the avocado cream if you prefer (see page 52).

FROM THE GROCER

50 g (1¾ oz) butter

50 g (1¾ oz/¼ cup) quinoa

salt and freshly ground black pepper

1 litre (34 fl oz/4 cups) chicken stock

60 ml (2 fl oz/¼ cup) sherry vinegar

75 ml (2½ fl oz) pouring (single/light) cream

25 ml (¾ fl oz) olive oil

FROM THE GREENGROCER

1 large onion, finely chopped

100 g (3½ oz) potatoes, peeled and diced

1 red capsicum (bell pepper), halved, seeded and diced

2 red chillies, halved, seeded and finely shredded, plus extra to garnish

450 g (1 lb/2¼ cups) corn kernels

juice of 3 limes

1 bunch of coriander (cilantro), roughly chopped, plus extra leaves to garnish

1 large avocado

Melt the butter in a large saucepan over a medium–low heat and add the onion, potatoes, red capsicum and chillies. Stir and add a little water. Cover and let the vegetables sweat for about 15 minutes. Add a splash more water every so often to keep the mixture moist.

Meanwhile, put the quinoa into a dry frying pan and toast over a medium heat for about 3 minutes, or until the grains darken slightly and start to pop. Remove from the heat and set aside.

Add the corn, salt and pepper, and chicken stock to the pan with the vegetables, followed by the toasted quinoa. Simmer for 15–20 minutes but don't overcook or the quinoa will go mushy. Add two-thirds of the lime juice and the chopped coriander. Thin the soup with extra stock or water if needed.

To make the avocado cream, simply scoop the avocado flesh into a food processor and add the vinegar, remaining lime juice, cream and olive oil. Proccess to a smooth purée. Taste for seasoning – you may wish to add more lime or salt and pepper. Serve the soup hot, drizzled with the avocado cream. Garnish with coriander leaves and shredded chilli.

JERUSALEM ARTICHOKE, SPELT & HAZELNUT SOUP

This soup is very earthy and full of the flavours of autumn. If you want a chunkier soup, don't purée it but mash lightly with a potato masher or the back of a wooden spoon to break the ingredients down a little.

FROM THE GROCER

75 g (2¾ oz) butter

salt and freshly ground black pepper

850 ml (28½ fl oz) chicken or vegetable stock

200 ml (7 fl oz) milk

50 g (1¾ oz) hazelnuts, toasted and very roughly chopped, plus extra to serve

40 g (1½ oz) spelt

75 ml (2½ fl oz) thick (double/heavy) cream

FROM THE GREENGROCER

1 leek, white part only, sliced

½ onion, finely chopped

700 g (1 lb 9 oz) Jerusalem artichokes

flat-leaf (Italian) parsley, roughly chopped, to serve

Melt the butter in a heavy-based saucepan over a medium–low heat and add the leek, onion and a splash of water. Cover and sweat the vegetables while you prepare the artichokes.

Wash the artichokes well in water; there is no need to peel them, just chop into small chunks and add to the saucepan with the leek and onion. Stir and season with salt and pepper. Cover the pan and sweat the vegetables further until the artichokes are just soft, about 10 minutes. Add the stock and cook until the mixture is very soft and mushy, about 15 minutes. Remove from the heat and then add the milk and hazelnuts. Leave to cool.

Place the spelt in a saucepan and cover with plenty of cold water. Bring to the boil, reduce the heat and simmer for 25 minutes. The spelt should be soft but still retain a little bite. Drain, season and set aside.

Transfer the cooled soup to a food processor and coarsely purée – it's nice to retain a little nutty crunch. Return the soup to the saucepan and add the cream. Reheat over a medium heat and add the spelt, adding more stock or water if you want the soup to have a thinner consistency. Taste and adjust the seasoning.

When the soup is hot, serve into bowls and scatter over some hazelnuts and parsley.

WHITE BEAN & SMOKED BACON SOUP

This is a very elegant soup despite being made from such rustic ingredients.

FROM THE GROCER

250 g (9 oz/1¼ cups) dried haricot (navy) beans or butterbeans, soaked overnight

6 cloves

1 dried bay leaf

8 black peppercorns

60 ml (2 fl oz/¼ cup) olive oil

1 litre (34 fl oz/4 cups) chicken or ham stock

150 ml (5 fl oz) pouring (single/light) cream (optional)

freshly ground black pepper

FROM THE GREENGROCER

2 onions, peeled

a handful of parsley stalks, plus chopped parsley, to serve (optional)

1 celery stalk, diced

2 small carrots, diced

FROM THE BUTCHER

200 g (7 oz) piece of smoked bacon, cut into cubes

Drain and rinse the beans, place them in a large saucepan and cover with 2 litres (68 fl oz/8 cups) cold water. Stick the cloves into 1 of the onions and add to the pan along with the bay leaf, parsley stalks and peppercorns. Bring to the boil, skim off any scum and then partially cover. Reduce the heat so the liquid is simmering and cook for a couple of hours, or until the beans are just tender. Keep an eye on the water level – you may need to add more liquid to prevent the beans drying out. When cooked, drain the beans and discard the onion, bay leaf and parsley stalks.

Finely chop the remaining onion. Heat the olive oil in a large saucepan over a medium heat and add the chopped onion, celery, carrots and bacon, reserving some of the bacon for a garnish. Cook gently until golden. Add the beans and the stock (if using ham stock make sure it's not too salty). Bring to the boil, then reduce the heat and simmer for 20–30 minutes, or until the beans collapse completely. Squash them with the back of a wooden spoon or use a potato masher to help them along if necessary. Add the cream (if using), pepper and taste for seasoning – you probably won't need salt. Quickly fry the remaining bacon in its own fat over a high heat.

Ladle the soup into bowls, divide the fried bacon between each serving and scatter with the parsley (if using).

PORCINI, CHICKEN & FARRO SOUP

This is a really good soup that can almost be made with pantry ingredients – you just need to shop for the fresh mushrooms.

FROM THE GROCER

20 g (¾ oz) dried porcini (cep) mushrooms

60 ml (2 fl oz/¼ cup) olive oil

salt and freshly ground black pepper

75 g (2¾ oz) farro

800 ml (27 fl oz) chicken stock

80 ml (2½ fl oz/⅓ cup) amontillado sherry, or other dry or medium sherry

crème fraîche (optional)

FROM THE GREENGROCER

250 g (9 oz) Swiss brown or chestnut mushrooms

½ onion, finely chopped

1 celery stalk, diced

1 carrot, diced

2 garlic cloves, finely chopped

chopped flat-leaf (Italian) parsley, to serve (optional)

FROM THE BUTCHER

150 g (5½ oz) cooked chicken, shredded

Cover the porcini mushrooms with 150 ml (5 fl oz) boiling water and leave for 1 hour, then drain through a sieve lined with muslin (cheesecloth) or a double layer of paper towel to collect any grit. Reserve the liquor and chop any large porcini mushrooms.

Cut any large Swiss brown mushrooms into smaller pieces. Heat 2 tablespoons of the olive oil in a frying pan over a medium–high heat and briskly cook the mushrooms until golden brown all over. Season.

Heat the remaining oil in a saucepan and add the onion, celery and carrot. Cook for about 2 minutes over a medium heat to get a little colour and then add the garlic and cook for another 2 minutes. Add the farro and stir until the grains are nice and glossy. Add the stock, the porcini mushrooms and their soaking liquor, and the Swiss brown mushrooms. Bring to the boil, reduce the heat and simmer for 40 minutes. The farro should be soft but still have a little bite. Add the sherry and the chicken and cook for another 2 minutes or so.

Serve scattered with the parsley (if using). If you are making this for a special occasion, a dollop of crème fraîche spooned on top of each serving is lovely.

HOT & SOUR CHICKEN SOUP
WITH ADZUKI BEANS, MUSHROOMS & SPINACH

If you have some left-over chicken and chicken stock to hand this is a cinch to make and so healthy you can almost feel it doing you good as you eat it.

FROM THE GROCER

2 litres (68 fl oz/8 cups) chicken stock

150 g (5½ oz) cooked adzuki beans, drained and rinsed

1½ tablespoons fish sauce

1½ teaspoons soft light brown sugar

FROM THE GREENGROCER

1 lemongrass stem, white part only, finely shredded

2.5 cm (1 in) cube fresh ginger, finely shredded

8 spring onions (scallions), trimmed and chopped

1 small carrot, julienned

2 red chillies, halved, seeded and thinly sliced

80 g (2¾ oz) button, Swiss brown, chestnut or shiitake mushrooms, sliced

100 g (3½ oz/2¼ cups) baby English spinach leaves, shredded

2 tablespoons roughly chopped coriander (cilantro) leaves

juice of ½ lime

FROM THE BUTCHER

250 g (9 oz) boneless, skinless chicken breasts or thighs, cut into thin strips

Put the chicken stock into a saucepan and add the lemongrass, ginger, spring onions, carrot and chillies. Bring to the boil, then reduce the heat and simmer for 10 minutes.

Add the mushrooms, chicken, beans, fish sauce and sugar to the stock and simmer for about 3 minutes, or until the chicken is cooked through. Stir in the spinach, coriander and lime juice. Taste and add more lime juice, sugar or fish sauce if you wish.

salads

MANGO, ASPARAGUS & WILD RICE SALAD

To make this even more substantial you can add chargrilled chicken or flaked cooked salmon.

FROM THE GROCER

50 g (1¾ oz/¼ cup) wild rice

100 g (3½ oz/½ cup) long-grain brown rice

275 ml (9½ fl oz) chicken or vegetable stock

1½ teaspoons apple cider vinegar

¼ teaspoon dijon mustard

1½ teaspoons honey

2 tablespoons peanut oil

2 tablespoons olive oil

salt and freshly ground black pepper

FROM THE GREENGROCER

1 red chilli, halved, seeded and finely shredded

175 g (6 oz) green beans, trimmed and cut in half

450 g (1 lb) asparagus, medium rather than thick spears

2 tablespoons roughly chopped coriander (cilantro) leaves

1 mango, peeled and sliced

Cook both kinds of rice together in the stock. Wild rice never really softens but stays firm and nutty; brown rice softens but not as much as white rice. The rice should cook in around 40 minutes and absorb all the stock as it cooks – but make sure it doesn't boil dry. Add a little water as and when needed.

While the rice is cooking, make the dressing by whisking together the vinegar, mustard, honey, chilli, peanut and olive oils, and salt and pepper.

Cook the beans in boiling salted water until al dente. Drain the beans and then plunge them into ice-cold water so they stay bright green. Trim the base of each asparagus spear and peel away any tough skin. Boil or steam the asparagus until just tender – about 4 minutes – and then plunge these into cold water too. Drain.

Mix the rice, beans, asparagus, coriander and mango together and toss with the dressing.

ROAST TOMATO, RICOTTA & BLACK BELUGA LENTIL SALAD

The colours here – red, black and white – make this salad look beautiful. It will seem like you have a lot of tomatoes when you start but they shrink a lot.

FROM THE GROCER

65 ml (2¼ fl oz) olive oil

1 teaspoon harissa

2¼ teaspoons caster (superfine) sugar, plus an extra pinch

salt and freshly ground black pepper

1 tablespoon white wine vinegar

1 teaspoon dijon mustard

80 ml (2½ fl oz/⅓ cup) extra-virgin olive oil, plus extra for drizzling

115 g (4 oz) black beluga lentils, rinsed and drained

125 g (4½ oz/½ cup) ricotta, broken into walnut-sized nuggets

FROM THE GREENGROCER

12 roma (plum) tomatoes, halved

½ small white onion, finely chopped

½ celery stalk, finely chopped

1 tablespoon finely chopped flat-leaf (Italian) parsley

1 tablespoon finely chopped mint

¼ small red onion, sliced wafer-thin

Preheat the oven to 160°C (320°F). Lay the tomatoes in a single layer on one large or two small roasting tins. Mix together 2½ tablespoons of the olive oil and all of the harissa, pour this over the tomatoes and turn them over with your hands to coat well. Arrange the tomatoes cut-side up, sprinkle with the sugar and season with salt and pepper. Roast for 45 minutes, or until the tomatoes have caramelised and are slightly shrunken. Leave to cool a little.

Make the dressing by whisking together the vinegar, mustard, extra-virgin olive oil, the pinch of sugar and salt and pepper. Set aside.

Place the lentils in a saucepan, cover with cold water and bring to the boil. Reduce the heat and simmer until the lentils are tender but still hold their shape, about 15–20 minutes. Meanwhile, heat the remaining olive oil in a frying pan over a low heat and gently sauté the white onion and celery until soft but not coloured. Drain the lentils and add to the sautéed vegetables, stirring to coat in the cooking juices. Add the dressing, parsley and mint and season well. Gently stir in the red onion.

Transfer the lentils to a serving platter and scatter the roasted tomatoes and the ricotta on top. Drizzle over some extra-virgin olive oil and grind black pepper over the top. Serve warm or at room temperature.

MINTED PEA, BROAD BEAN & EDAMAME SALAD

This is the simplest, most summery salad. You can make a similar version by replacing the feta cheese with chorizo or bacon lardons (just sauté in hot oil) or flaked cooked salmon or crab.

FROM THE GROCER

2 tablespoons extra-virgin olive oil

salt and freshly ground black pepper

125 g (4½ oz) feta cheese, crumbled

FROM THE GREENGROCER

250 g (9 oz) fresh or frozen broad (fava) beans (podded weight)

150 g (5½ oz) edamame (podded weight)

250 g (9 oz) fresh or frozen peas (podded weight)

juice of ½ lemon

2 tablespoons chopped mint

If you are using frozen broad beans, cook all the beans and peas together in boiling salted water until tender. If you are using fresh broad beans, give them a couple of minutes' head start and then add the peas and edamame. Drain and run under cold water to preserve their colour. Slip the skins off the broad beans – it is a bit of a hassle but the colour inside is gorgeous – and discard the skins.

Put the peas and beans into a broad shallow bowl with the olive oil, lemon juice, mint and salt and pepper. Scatter over the feta, gently fork it through and serve.

SALMON, AVOCADO & BEAN SALAD
WITH MANGO, CHILLI & LIME DRESSING

Beautiful looking, this salad is very healthy too. If you want to ring the changes, replace the mango with pink grapefruit – this also makes a very pretty dish. A salad of brown rice, or some vinegared sushi rice is lovely served alongside.

FROM THE GROCER

60 ml (2 fl oz/¼ cup) rice vinegar

60 ml (2 fl oz/¼ cup) light olive oil

1½ tablespoons caster (superfine) sugar, or to taste

salt and freshly ground pepper

FROM THE GREENGROCER

juice of 3 limes

zest of 1 lime

2.5 cm (1 in) cube fresh ginger, finely grated

1 garlic clove, crushed

1 red chilli, halved, seeded and very thinly sliced

2 ripe avocados

1 just-ripe mango

150 g (5½ oz) podded edamame

100 g (3½ oz) watercress, thick stalks removed

15 g (½ oz/½ cup) coriander (cilantro) leaves

50 g (1¾ oz) pea shoots

FROM THE FISHMONGER

600 g (1 lb 5 oz) salmon fillets, skinned, pin-boned and very thinly sliced

To make the dressing, mix together the vinegar, the juice of 1 lime, the lime zest, ginger, garlic, chilli, olive oil, 2½ teaspoons of the caster sugar and salt and pepper. Set aside.

For the salad, place the salmon in a large shallow bowl with the remaining lime juice, remaining sugar and salt and pepper. Toss the fish in the marinade and remove it immediately, or leave to marinate for 5–15 minutes before mixing it with the rest of the salad.

Halve the avocados and remove the stones. Cut each half into slices, then peel the skin from each slice as neatly as possible. Peel the mango and cut the cheek from each side of the stone. Cut the cheeks into very thin and neat slices.

Steam or boil the edamame for 3 minutes and rinse with cold water. Gently toss the edamame, avocado, watercress, coriander and pea shoots together with two-thirds of the dressing. Arrange the salad on individual plates or in a broad shallow serving dish and lay the slices of mango and salmon on top. Drizzle on the rest of the dressing, grind some black pepper over the top and serve immediately.

TUNA, ANCHOVY, SEMI-DRIED TOMATO & CANNELLINI BEAN SALAD

This is a great pantry standby. Borlotti (cranberry) or flageolet beans can be used instead of cannellini (lima) beans and dried or fresh cherry tomatoes can replace semi-dried (sun-blushed). The onion – and even the anchovies – can be left out altogether. Use good-quality tuna, olives and oil.

FROM THE GROCER

1 x 250 g (9 oz) tin tuna in olive oil, drained and roughly broken up

2 x 400 g (14 oz) tins cannellini (lima) beans, drained and rinsed

75 g (2¾ oz) semi-dried (sun-blushed) tomatoes

16 anchovies packed in salt or olive oil, drained and chopped

about 50 black olives in olive oil, pitted and halved

salt and freshly ground black pepper

180 ml (6 fl oz) extra-virgin olive oil

2 teaspoons dijon mustard

FROM THE GREENGROCER

1 small red onion, very thinly sliced

3 tablespoons chopped flat-leaf (Italian) parsley

juice of 1 lemon

Put the tuna, beans, tomatoes, anchovies, onion, olives and parsley together in a bowl. Season well with salt and pepper. In a teacup, mix the olive oil, mustard and lemon juice together. Season and check to see whether your balance of lemon to oil is good – remember you are going to add this to something very starchy so it needs a bit of tang. Pour the dressing over the bean and tuna mixture, being careful not to squash the beans. Taste for seasoning and adjust as necessary.

CHARGRILLED FENNEL & CHICORY
WITH WHEAT GRAIN, GOAT'S CHEESE & PINE NUTS

This is Sicilian-inspired as it plays with bitter, savoury and sweet flavours in the same dish. Do try to get red chicory (endive) if you can – it's a lovely colour with the other ingredients.

FROM THE GROCER

1 tablespoon balsamic vinegar, plus an extra slug

75 ml (2½ fl oz) extra-virgin olive oil

salt and freshly ground black pepper

75 g (2¾ oz) wheat grain (wheat berry), soaked overnight, drained and rinsed

40 g (1½ oz/⅓ cup) raisins

60–80 ml (2–2½ fl oz/¼–⅓ cup) olive oil, plus extra for brushing

25 g (1 oz) pine nuts, toasted

125 g (4½ oz) goat's cheese, crumbled

FROM THE GREENGROCER

a squeeze of lemon

4 heads of red chicory (endive)

2 fennel bulbs, tough outer leaves removed, ends trimmed, quartered lengthways

2 tablespoons coarsely chopped flat-leaf (Italian) parsley

Make the dressing by mixing together 1 tablespoon of the balsamic vinegar, extra-virgin olive oil, squeeze of lemon and salt and pepper. Set aside.

Cover the wheat grain with cold water in a saucepan. Bring to the boil, then reduce the heat and cook for 1 hour–1 hour 15 minutes. The grains should be soft but not mushy. Immediately drain and toss with half the dressing. Season well and set aside.

Meanwhile, put the raisins in a small saucepan and add just enough water to cover. Bring to the boil, then turn the heat off and let the raisins soak for about 15 minutes.

Pour 60–80 ml (2–2½ fl oz/¼–⅓ cup) of the olive oil into a shallow dish and add the slug of balsamic vinegar and salt and pepper to make a marinade. Quarter each chicory head and immediately place in the marinade, turning to lightly coat. Set aside.

Cook the fennel in gently boiling water for 4 minutes, or until tender. Remove and drain well.

Heat a chargrill pan until very hot. Brush the fennel with olive oil and chargrill on both sides until lightly charred. Set aside in a bowl. Chargrill the chicory until softened on the outside but still quite firm on the inside. Add to the bowl with the fennel and gently toss through the parsley and remaining dressing.

Place the wheat grain in a shallow serving bowl or divide between four plates. Add the chicory and fennel. Drain the raisins and scatter over the top with the pine nuts and goat's cheese.

A wide variety of seeds, pulses and grains are suitable for sprouting, and can be eaten raw in salads (a mixture is good) or cooked. Grain sprouts like wheat, barley or rye can be used in breads or stir-fries.

how to
SPROUT SEEDS, PULSES & GRAINS

1 Soak your chosen seeds, pulses or grains overnight in plenty of cold water.

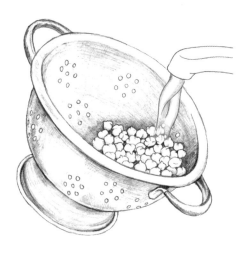

2 Rinse really well in a colander or fine sieve. Grains have to be especially well rinsed, as they will develop a gelatinous coating.

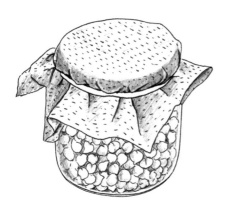

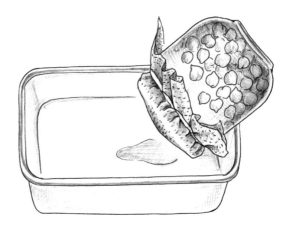

3 Place a couple of tablespoons of the rinsed seeds or 50 g (1¾ oz) of the pulses or grains in a clean jam jar and cover with muslin (cheesecloth), securing the fabric tightly around the neck of the jar with a rubber band.

4 Set the jar at an angle in a small tray or bowl and leave out of direct sunlight.

5 Carefully rinse the jar and its contents twice a day to prevent mould from growing, replacing the fabric and returning the jar to its angled position each time.

6 Depending on what you are sprouting, you should start to see little shoots after 2–3 days, and they can keep growing for up to 8 days if you want the sprouts to be long. Once your sprouts are ready, you can keep them in a sealed container in the refrigerator for a couple of weeks.

QUINOA, BLACK LENTIL, PUMPKIN & SPINACH SALAD

This is one of the prettiest dishes in this book – the colours are stunning.

FROM THE GROCER

50 g (1¾ oz) sultanas (golden raisins)

salt and freshly ground black pepper

2 tablespoons olive oil

200 g (7 oz) black lentils, rinsed and drained

200 g (7 oz/1 cup) quinoa

1 tablespoon white wine vinegar

2 teaspoons honey

80 ml (2½ fl oz/⅓ cup) rapeseed oil

¼ teaspoon garam masala

½ teaspoon korma curry powder

60 ml (2 fl oz/¼ cup) pouring (single/light) cream

FROM THE GREENGROCER

500 g (1 lb 2 oz) peeled and seeded pumpkin (winter squash)

35 g (1¼ oz/¾ cup) baby English spinach leaves

Preheat the oven to 180°C (350°F). Cover the sultanas with boiling water and leave to plump up for 20 minutes or so, then drain well. Meanwhile, cut the pumpkin into chunks and put into a roasting tin. Season with salt and pepper and drizzle with the olive oil. Roast for 20–30 minutes, or until completely tender.

Put the lentils in a saucepan and cover with water. Bring to the boil and cook for 15–30 minutes, or until tender but not falling apart. Drain and rinse. Cook the quinoa in boiling water for 15 minutes then drain.

To make the dressing, mix the vinegar with the honey, rapeseed oil, garam masala, curry powder, salt and pepper and cream. Stir in the drained sultanas. Toss the lentils and quinoa together and gently stir through the spinach, pumpkin and dressing. Serve immediately.

BUCKWHEAT & SALMON SALAD
WITH BEETROOT & SPINACH

This salad is astonishingly speedy to put together as you can cook buckwheat so quickly. Use smoked trout if you prefer and you can replace the beetroot (beet) with chopped cucumber.

FROM THE GROCER
400 g (14 oz) buckwheat
105 ml (3½ fl oz) rapeseed oil
salt and freshly ground black pepper
2 tablespoons extra-virgin olive oil
50 ml (1¾ fl oz) buttermilk

FROM THE GREENGROCER
juice of 1 lemon
1 small beetroot (beet), about 200 g
(7 oz), peeled and grated
50 g (1¾ oz) baby English
spinach leaves, torn
15 g (½ oz/¼ cup) chopped dill

FROM THE FISHMONGER
225 g (8 oz) hot smoked salmon

Place the buckwheat in a saucepan, cover with water and bring to the boil. Reduce the heat and simmer for 15 minutes. Drain and rinse. While the buckwheat is still warm dress it with 80 ml (2½ fl oz/⅓ cup) of the rapeseed oil and the lemon juice. Season with salt and pepper.

When the buckwheat is at room temperature gently toss it with the beetroot, spinach, salmon, dill and the rest of the rapeseed oil. Quickly mix together the extra-virgin olive oil, buttermilk and more seasoning. Drizzle over the salad and serve.

QUICK IDEAS

whip up a grain salad

Green spring spelt salad

Cook 200 g (7 oz) spelt in boiling water. Drain and rinse. Dress with 1 crushed garlic clove, grated zest of 1 lemon, juice of ½ lemon, 60 ml (2 fl oz/¼ cup) extra-virgin olive oil, salt and pepper. Stir in 2 tablespoons each of chopped flat-leaf (Italian) parsley and mint, 2 chopped spring onions (scallions), 25 g (1 oz) chopped pistachio nuts and a large handful of pea shoots.

Autumnal wild & brown rice salad

Cook 200 g (7 oz) mixed brown and wild rice. Drain and dress with 2¼ teaspoons balsamic vinegar, 1 teaspoon honey, 1 teaspoon dijon mustard, 60 ml (2 fl oz/¼ cup) walnut oil, 1 tablespoon extra-virgin olive oil and salt and pepper. Add 2 tablespoons each dried cranberries, dried chopped apples and raisins that have been soaked in boiling water for 15 minutes and drained; 25 g (1 oz) chopped hazelnuts, zest of 1 orange and 1 tablespoon pumpkin seeds (pepitas).

Fruity & summery couscous salad

Pour 200 ml (7 fl oz) boiling water and 2 tablespoons olive oil over 200 g (7 oz) wholemeal (whole-wheat) couscous. Leave for 15 minutes, then stir with a fork. Mix together 1 tablespoon lemon juice, 60 ml (2 fl oz/¼ cup) extra-virgin olive oil, 1 teaspoon honey, 1 teaspoon wholegrain mustard, and toss through the couscous. Season. Add 2 tablespoons chopped mint, 2 tablespoons toasted pine nuts, chopped flesh of 1 nectarine and 150 g (5½ oz) chopped tomatoes.

Hot Moroccan farro salad

Cook 200 g (7 oz) farro for about 20–30 minutes, drain and rinse. Mix the juice of 1 lemon, 100 ml (3½ fl oz) extra-virgin olive oil, ½ teaspoon each ground cumin, cayenne and salt and pepper. Stir into the farro with 100 g (3½ oz) chopped green olives, thinly sliced ¼ red onion, 100 g (3½ oz) drained chickpeas (garbanzo beans),100 g (3½ oz) crumbled feta cheese, 150 g (5½ oz) chopped tomatoes, 15 g (½ oz/¼ cup) chopped coriander (cilantro) and chopped rind of ½ preserved lemon.

Smoky kamut salad

Cook 200 g (7 oz) kamut in boiling water for 50 minutes. Drain and rinse, season well and dress with 2 tablespoons white balsamic vinegar, 100 ml (3½ fl oz) pumpkin seed (pepita) oil and 1 tablespoon maple syrup. Add 125 g (4½ oz) sliced smoked chicken, 15 g (½ oz) chopped smoked almonds, 1 thinly sliced pear tossed in the juice of 1 lemon, 1 thinly sliced red chicory (endive), and 1½ teaspoons pumpkin seeds (pepitas).

Harissa-spiced quinoa salad

Cook 150 g (5½ oz/¾ cup) quinoa in water for 15 minutes then drain and rinse. Dress with juice of 1 lemon mixed with 60 ml (2 fl oz/ ¼ cup) extra-virgin olive oil and 1 teaspoon harissa. Gently mix in 2 sliced avocados; 150 g (5½ oz) halved cherry tomatoes; 1 red chilli, halved, seeded and thinly sliced; 4 chopped spring onions (scallions); 1 tablespoon pumpkin seeds (pepitas); 1½ teaspoons chia seeds; 2 tablespoons chopped coriander (cilantro) leaves; salt and pepper.

WINTER GRAIN & VEGETABLE SALAD
WITH HONEY & MUSTARD DRESSING

This seems very frugal as you read the ingredients but is actually one of the most useful salads in this book. Serve with cheeses and bread for a simple lunch. Use spelt, farro or barley instead of wheat grain – just be sure to cook your grain of choice for the right amount of time.

FROM THE GROCER

100 g (3½ oz) wheat grain (wheat berry), soaked in water overnight, drained and rinsed

1 teaspoon wholegrain mustard

2 teaspoons runny honey

25 ml (¾ fl oz) apple cider vinegar

salt and freshly ground black pepper

120 ml (4 fl oz) extra-virgin olive oil (a fruity one if possible)

1 teaspoon ginger syrup from a jar of stem ginger (optional)

2¼ teaspoons mixed seeds such as hemp, sesame, pumpkin (pepitas) and sunflower kernels

FROM THE GREENGROCER

½ red chilli, seeded and shredded

2 garlic cloves, crushed

300 g (10½ oz) celeriac

juice of ½ lemon

2 carrots, peeled

1 cauliflower, broken into small florets

12 French breakfast radishes, trimmed and sliced wafer-thin

400 g (14 oz) baby English spinach leaves

100 g watercress

Place the wheat grain in a saucepan and cover with plenty of cold water. Bring to the boil then reduce the heat to a simmer and cook for 1 hour 15 minutes, or until the grains are just tender. Drain and set aside.

Meanwhile, to make the dressing, put the mustard, honey, vinegar and salt and pepper into a cup or small pitcher. Using a fork, whisk in the oil in a steady stream. Now stir in the ginger syrup (if using), the chilli and garlic. Taste for seasoning and set aside.

Peel the celeriac and then, using a vegetable peeler, peel off broad ribbons and immediately place them in a bowl of water spiked with the lemon juice. Peel ribbons of carrot in the same way – it's not necessary to soak these – and mix together with the cauliflower, radishes, spinach, cress and seeds. Drain the celeriac, pat dry and add to the bowl. Toss together with the wheat grain and the dressing. Serve immediately.

SMOKED HADDOCK, BARLEY & SPINACH SALAD

This is a very gutsy salad, good in the autumn and winter. Smoked mackerel – which is already cooked of course – is good instead of haddock. If you want to make this more substantial, a poached egg is lovely on top of each serving.

FROM THE GROCER

25 g (1 oz) dijon mustard

100 ml (3½ fl oz) white wine vinegar

salt and freshly ground black pepper

1 teaspoon caster (superfine) sugar

180 ml (6 fl oz) light and fruity extra-virgin olive oil

75 ml (2½ fl oz) pouring (single/light) cream

220 g (8 oz/1 cup) pearl barley

2 tablespoons olive oil

25 g (1 oz) butter

1 tablespoon sunflower oil

FROM THE GREENGROCER

a good squeeze of lemon

1 tablespoon chopped flat-leaf (Italian) parsley

250 g (9 oz) slim or medium leeks, white part only, washed

350 g (12½ oz) baby English spinach leaves

chives to serve (optional)

FROM THE FISHMONGER

1 kg (2 lb 3 oz) smoked haddock fillet (undyed), skin on, bones removed, cut into 6 portions

To make the dressing, put the mustard, vinegar, salt and pepper and sugar into a small pitcher and gradually add the extra-virgin olive oil, whisking with a fork as you go. Stir in the cream and taste for seasoning.

Cook the barley in lightly salted boiling water until tender, about 30 minutes. Drain, rinse in warm water and drain again, shaking out any excess liquid. Transfer to a warm bowl and stir in the olive oil, squeeze of lemon and salt and pepper. Cover to keep warm.

Steam the leeks until tender when pierced with the tip of a knife. If your leeks are very small, use them whole. If using larger leeks cut them into 8 cm (3¼ in) lengths. Add them to the bowl with the barley and toss through the spinach and about three-quarters of the dressing. The mixture should be well moistened but not drowning in dressing, so add it gradually. Check for seasoning.

Heat the butter and sunflower oil in two frying pans and cook three pieces of fish in each, flesh side down, over a medium heat until pale golden underneath, about 2 minutes. Turn the fish over, reduce the heat a little and cover both pans. Cook for about 5 minutes, or until the flesh is opaque. Take the pans off the heat.

Divide the salad between six plates or transfer to a wide shallow serving bowl. Lift the fish flesh off the skin in fairly big chunks and set on top of the salad. Drizzle over the rest of the dressing. Scatter chopped chives on top (if using) and serve immediately.

DUCK & WILD RICE SALAD
WITH CRANBERRIES & SPICED PECANS

Plain chicken – fried in a chargrill pan or left-over roasted – also works well in this very American salad. Change the cranberries to dried sour cherries too, if you like.

FROM THE GROCER

35 g (1¼ oz/⅓ cup) pecans

25 g (1 oz) butter

½ teaspoon mixed (pumpkin pie) spice

¼ teaspoon cayenne pepper

60 g (2 oz/⅓ cup, lightly packed) soft dark brown sugar

salt and freshly ground black pepper

75 g (2¾ oz) wild rice

75 g (2¾ oz) brown basmati rice

300 ml (10 fl oz) chicken stock

1½ teaspoons apple cider vinegar

¼ teaspoon dijon mustard

1½ teaspoons maple syrup

2 tablespoons peanut oil

2 tablespoons extra-virgin olive oil

80 g (2¾ oz) dried cranberries, soaked in boiling water for 15 minutes, then drained

FROM THE BUTCHER

500 g (1 lb 2 oz) smoked duck, cut into neat slices

FROM THE GREENGROCER

5 g (¼ oz) chopped flat-leaf (Italian) parsley

150 g (5½ oz/5 cups) watercress

Put the pecans into a dry frying pan over a high heat and toast for about 30 seconds, then add the butter, mixed spice, cayenne pepper and sugar. Reduce the heat and cook for another 1½–2 minutes, turning the nuts over as you go – they should be caramelised but be careful not to burn them. Season lightly with salt and pepper and spread out on a plate to cool.

Put both types of rice into a saucepan and cover with the stock. Bring to the boil, season and then reduce the heat to a simmer. Cook until all the stock has been absorbed and the rice is tender, about 35 minutes. If it gets too dry add a little water. Wild rice never goes soft – it remains firm and nutty.

While the rice is cooking, make the dressing by whisking together the vinegar, mustard, maple syrup, peanut oil and extra-virgin olive oil. Taste for seasoning.

As soon as the rice is ready, pour over half the dressing and mix. Leave to cool to room temperature and taste for seasoning – rice salad needs a lot. Gently mix in the duck, parsley, watercress and cranberries. Add the pecans and the rest of the dressing. Taste again for seasoning and serve.

CERVELLE DE CANUT
WITH LENTIL SALAD

Cervelle de canut is lovely to have in the refrigerator because it's light and fresh. To make this more substantial you could add cooked wheat grain (wheat berry) to the lentils and slivers of tomato.

FROM THE GROCER

200 g (7 oz) fromage blanc

75 g (2¾ oz) soft goat's cheese

100 g (3½ oz) crème fraîche

1½ teaspoons white wine vinegar

1 tablespoon dry white wine

75 ml (2½ fl oz) extra-virgin olive oil, plus extra for drizzling

salt and freshly ground black pepper

½ teaspoon dijon mustard

¾ teaspoon sherry vinegar

1½ teaspoons balsamic vinegar

1 tablespoon olive oil

250 g (9 oz) puy (tiny blue-green) lentils, rinsed and drained

1 dried bay leaf

FROM THE GREENGROCER

3½ garlic cloves

2½ tablespoons chopped flat-leaf (Italian) parsley

1 tablespoon finely chopped chives

1 tablespoon finely chopped chervil

1 onion, very finely chopped

1 celery stalk, very finely chopped

1 thyme sprig

a good squeeze of lemon

FROM THE BAKER

toasted sourdough or good baguette to serve

To make the cervelle de canut, mix together the fromage blanc, goat's cheese, crème fraîche, white wine vinegar, white wine, 1 tablespoon of the extra-virgin olive oil, 1½ of the garlic cloves (crushed), 1 tablespoon of the parsley, the chives, the chervil and salt and pepper. Gently mash the goat's cheese as you mix. Cover and chill overnight.

Make the vinaigrette by mixing together the mustard, sherry vinegar, balsamic vinegar, the remaining extra-virgin olive oil and more seasoning. Set aside.

For the lentils, heat the olive oil in a saucepan over a medium–low heat and gently sauté the onion and celery until soft but not coloured. Add the remaining 2 garlic cloves (finely chopped) and cook for another minute or so, then add the lentils and turn them over in the oil and vegetable juices. Add the thyme and the bay leaf. Pour in 650 ml (22 fl oz) water and season lightly. Bring to the boil, reduce the heat and simmer uncovered until just tender, about 15–25 minutes. By the time the lentils are cooked they should have absorbed all the liquid, but drain if there is any left.

Transfer the lentils to a bowl, pick out the bay and thyme, and add the lemon juice, remaining parsley and vinaigrette. Leave the lentils to cool and then check for moistness and seasoning. Divide between six plates and place a generous scoop of cervelle de canut on top, or serve on the side. Drizzle with a little extra-virgin olive oil and serve with the toasted bread.

CHORIZO, AVOCADO & CHICKPEAS
WITH SHERRY DRESSING

To make this a gutsier dish, top with a fried egg.

FROM THE GROCER

1 teaspoon sherry vinegar

100 ml (3½ fl oz) extra-virgin olive oil

2 teaspoons medium sherry

salt and freshly ground black pepper

1 tablespoon olive oil, plus extra
for drizzling

400 g (14 oz) tinned chickpeas
(garbanzo beans), drained and rinsed

FROM THE GREENGROCER

2 red capsicums (bell peppers),
halved and seeded

2 ripe avocados, halved and stones
removed

a squeeze of lemon

125 g (4½ oz) rocket (arugula), baby
English spinach leaves, watercress
or lamb's lettuce (corn salad/mâche)

FROM THE BUTCHER

225 g (8 oz) chorizo, peeled and
sliced into rounds

Preheat the oven to 190ºC (375ºF). Make the dressing by whisking together the vinegar, extra-virgin olive oil, sherry and salt and pepper. Set aside.

Drizzle the capsicums with a little olive oil, season and roast for about 30 minutes, or until soft, then cut into strips.

Cut the avocado halves in slices lengthways then carefully peel away the skin. Squeeze over a little lemon juice and season.

Heat the olive oil in a frying pan over a medium heat and quickly sauté the chorizo on both sides until golden.

Gently toss together the capsicum, avocado, chorizo, chickpeas, rocket and dressing and serve.

BUCKWHEAT & RED CABBAGE SALAD
WITH SOUR CHERRIES AND BLUE CHEESE

This is a good combination of earthy, sweet, salty and nutty. You can use a different grain if buckwheat doesn't appeal – this dish is also good made with kamut or wheat grain (wheat berry).

FROM THE GROCER

400 g (14 oz) buckwheat

½ teaspoon wholegrain mustard

½ teaspoon honey

salt and freshly ground black pepper

2 tablespoons white balsamic vinegar

2 tablespoons walnut oil

80 ml (2½ fl oz/⅓ cup) extra-virgin olive oil

50 g (1¾ oz) dried sour cherries

30 g (1 oz) toasted walnuts, chopped

125 g (4½ oz) blue cheese, crumbled

FROM THE GREENGROCER

½ red cabbage

2 tablespoons chopped flat-leaf (Italian) parsley

Put the buckwheat in a saucepan, cover with water and bring to the boil. Reduce the heat and simmer for 15 minutes. Drain and rinse. In a teacup, whisk together the mustard, honey, salt and pepper, balsamic vinegar and walnut and olive oils. While the buckwheat is still warm dress it with two-thirds of the vinaigrette and season well.

Put the dried cherries into a bowl, cover them with just-boiled water and leave to plump up for 15 minutes.

Cut the cabbage in half, remove the core and discard, then cut the cabbage into slices about 1 cm (½ in) thick.

Drain the cherries and toss them with the buckwheat along with the cabbage, walnuts, parsley and blue cheese, plus the rest of the dressing. Be careful not to squash the cheese too much when you are tossing everything together. Taste for seasoning and add another splash of balsamic vinegar if you think it needs it.

stews

INDIAN PUMPKIN & CHICKPEAS
WITH RAISINS & ALMONDS

If you want to go the healthy route, leave out the cream here or add a little yoghurt instead. If you use yoghurt, stir it in at the end or it will split when boiled.

FROM THE GROCER

2 tablespoons peanut or sunflower oil, plus extra for drizzling

salt and freshly ground black pepper

1 teaspoon ground cumin

400 ml (13½ fl oz) chicken or vegetable stock

50 g (1¾ oz) raisins

400 g (14 oz) tinned chickpeas (garbanzo beans), drained and rinsed

2 tablespoons ground almonds

20 g (¾ oz) desiccated (shredded) coconut

50 ml (1¾ fl oz) thick (double/heavy) cream

2 tablespoons flaked almonds, toasted

FROM THE GREENGROCER

1 kg (2 lb 3 oz) butternut pumpkin (squash), peeled, seeded and cut into large chunks

1 large onion, roughly chopped

3 garlic cloves, crushed

1 red chilli, halved, seeded and shredded

200 g (7 oz) cherry tomatoes

a generous squeeze of lime

1½ tablespoons chopped coriander (cilantro) leaves

Preheat the oven to 200ºC (400ºF). Place the pumpkin in a roasting tin, drizzle with peanut oil and season with salt and pepper. Roast for 15 minutes, or until the pumpkin has taken on a good colour.

Heat the 2 tablespoons of peanut oil in a large saucepan over a medium heat and cook the onion until soft and golden. Add the garlic and cook for another couple of minutes. Add the cumin and chilli and cook for a couple of minutes more to allow the flavours to release, then add the tomatoes and salt and pepper. Stir well to ensure the tomatoes are well coated in cooking juices and spice.

Add the pumpkin, with any juices from the roasting tin, plus the stock, raisins and chickpeas. Bring to the boil, immediately reduce the heat to medium and cook for 15 minutes, or until the pumpkin is completely tender. Stir in the ground almonds, coconut and cream, and heat through over a medium–low heat. Add the squeeze of lime and the coriander and check the seasoning; this dish can take quite a lot of salt but how much you need depends on the saltiness of the stock.

Scatter with the almond flakes and serve with rice.

CASSOULET

This is a relatively inexpensive version of cassoulet as it doesn't contain any duck confit. Be really generous with the seasoning and herbs – this dish contains a lot of beans and really needs assertive flavouring.

FROM THE GROCER

900 g (2 lb/4½ cups) dried haricot (navy) beans, soaked overnight and drained

6 cloves

salt and freshly ground black pepper

2 tablespoons tomato passata (puréed tomatoes)

80 g (2¾ oz) wholemeal breadcrumbs

FROM THE GREENGROCER

1 onion, peeled

1 bouquet garni

8 garlic cloves, crushed

10 roma (plum) tomatoes, roughly chopped

10 thyme sprigs, leaves only

10 g (¼ oz) roughly chopped flat-leaf (Italian) parsley

FROM THE BUTCHER

250 g (9 oz) piece streaky bacon, rind removed and reserved

800 g (1 lb 12 oz) boned breast of lamb

350 g (12½ oz) pork blade

225 g (8 oz) Toulouse sausages

Preheat the oven to 190°C (375°F). Put the beans in a saucepan and cover with plenty of cold water. Stick the cloves in the onion and add to the pan with the bacon rind, bouquet garni and half the garlic. Bring to the boil, skim off any scum, reduce the heat and cook slowly for about 1 hour 30 minutes. The cooking time will depend on the age of the beans, so it might take longer. Don't let the beans dry out.

While the beans are cooking, put the lamb, pork, bacon and sausages into a large roasting tin and roast for 30 minutes. When the meat is cooked, cut the sausages into thick slices and the other meat into 3 cm (1¼ in) cubes. Set aside. Reserve the fat in the tin.

When the beans are soft (but not falling apart) drain and reserve the cooking liquid. Discard the onion, bacon rind and bouquet garni. Turn the oven down to 170°C (340°F) and layer the components of the cassoulet in a heavy-based casserole: the beans, meat, roma tomatoes, remaining garlic and herbs. Season with salt and pepper as you go, and start and end with a layer of beans. Measure out 600 ml (20½ fl oz) of the bean cooking liquid and mix it with the tomato passata and reserved meat fat. Pour this into the casserole and sprinkle some of the breadcrumbs on top – don't use them all, as you will need more as the cassoulet cooks. Cover, transfer to the oven and bake for 1 hour 30 minutes. After 45 minutes take the lid off and stir to incorporate the breadcrumbs. Sprinkle over more breadcrumbs, cover and return to the oven.

Check the cassoulet about 20 minutes before it is due to be ready. It should be thick and oily, so judge whether you need to stir in the breadcrumbs from the top and add more. The breadcrumbs will help it thicken but only add more if you need to – you don't want the cassoulet to be dry. When you serve the cassoulet, it should have a layer of golden breadcrumbs on top.

SOBRONADE

This is like a lazy person's cassoulet – much quicker to make and with fewer ingredients – but still very satisfying.

FROM THE GROCER

60 g (2 oz) goose or duck fat

250 g (9 oz/1¼ cups) dried haricot (navy) beans, soaked overnight and drained

2 dried bay leaves

400 g (14 oz) tinned cherry tomatoes in thick juice

salt and freshly ground black pepper

2 teaspoons soft light brown sugar

FROM THE GREENGROCER

2 large onions, peeled

3 large carrots, cut into 2 cm (¾ in) dice

500 g (1 lb 2 oz) celeriac, peeled and cut into 2 cm (¾ in) dice

300 g (10½ oz) turnips or swedes (rutabagas), peeled and cut into 2 cm (¾ in) dice

6 garlic cloves, crushed

6 thyme sprigs, leaves removed

a small bunch of flat-leaf (Italian) parsley, leaves picked, plus 1 tablespoon chopped leaves to serve

300 g (10½ oz) waxy potatoes, cut into chunks

FROM THE BUTCHER

500 g (1 lb 2 oz) skinned and boned pork belly, cut into 2 cm (¾ in) cubes

800 g (1 lb 12 oz) Toulouse sausages

Heat 1 tablespoon of the goose fat in a large heavy-based flameproof casserole dish over a high heat. Brown the pork all over, then add the beans. Quarter 1 of the onions and add to the dish. Cover with water, bring to the boil and then reduce the heat. Skim off any scum, cover and simmer while you cook the vegetables.

Roughly chop the remaining onion and heat 2 tablespoons of the fat in a frying pan over a medium heat. Working in batches, fry the chopped onion, carrots, celeriac and turnips or swedes until golden but not cooked through. As each batch is finished, add to the casserole with the pork and beans. Add the garlic, thyme and bay leaves. Chop the parsley stalks and add them as well. Stir everything together, cover and simmer for 1 hour, stirring from time to time.

Brown the Toulouse sausages in the remaining fat until golden. Cut the sausages into chunks and add to the casserole along with the potatoes and tomatoes. Roughly chop the parsley leaves and add to the casserole with the salt and pepper and the sugar. Cover and simmer for 45 minutes, stirring from time to time. The cooking juices should have reduced and the beans become tender, producing a thick stew. If the mixture is too thin, continue cooking, stirring a little to crush the beans to help it thicken. Check for seasoning. Serve scattered with the 1 tablespoon of chopped parsley.

VERMONT BAKED BEANS
WITH BACON, MOLASSES & MAPLE SYRUP

If you don't have tomato passata (puréed tomatoes) use 125 g (4½ oz/½ cup) of tinned cherry tomatoes in thick juice.

FROM THE GROCER

500 g (1 lb 2 oz) haricot (navy) beans, soaked overnight and drained

8 cloves

120 ml (4 fl oz) tomato passata (puréed tomatoes)

60 ml (2 fl oz/¼ cup) maple syrup

60 ml (2 fl oz/¼ cup) molasses

25 g (1 oz) English mustard powder

60 ml (2 fl oz/¼ cup) apple cider vinegar

2 dried bay leaves

salt and freshly ground black pepper

FROM THE GREENGROCER

3 onions, quartered

4 garlic cloves, finely chopped

4 thyme sprigs

2 tablespoons roughly chopped flat-leaf (Italian) parsley

FROM THE BUTCHER

500 g (1 lb 2 oz) piece of smoked bacon, rind removed, cut into 2.5 cm (1 in) cubes

Put the beans into a heavy-based flameproof casserole dish with 1 of the quartered onions and enough water to cover by about 5 cm (2 in). Bring to the boil, reduce the heat and simmer, covered, for 1 hour. Make sure the beans are always immersed in liquid – top up with water if necessary.

Preheat the oven to 140°C (275°F). Stick the cloves into the remaining onion quarters. Add these to the bean dish along with all the other ingredients except the parsley. Don't season with salt yet – wait to see how salty the beans become with the bacon – but add plenty of pepper. Add more water if necessary to ensure the beans are covered. Bring to the boil again, cover and transfer to the oven. Cook for 1 hour 30 minutes. Keep an eye on the beans during this time and stir them every so often to keep them moist. Remove the lid and cook for a further 30 minutes. During this final cooking time the mixture should become darker and thicker. Check the seasoning and stir in the parsley. Serve hot straight from the casserole dish.

TAGINE OF LAMB
WITH CHICKPEAS, APRICOTS, SAFFRON & HONEY

Chickpeas are the main pulse used in Moroccan cookery but you can use other beans here such as haricot (navy) or cannellini (lima). This dish combines a delicious blend of sweet and savoury flavours imbued with saffron.

FROM THE GROCER

80 ml (2½ fl oz/⅓ cup) olive oil

15 g (½ oz) unsalted butter

1 teaspoon ground ginger

1 teaspoon ground cinnamon

salt and freshly ground black pepper

225 g (8 oz/1¼ cups) dried apricots

50 g (1¾ oz) dried barberries or sour cherries

800 ml (27 fl oz) lamb or chicken stock or water

a large pinch of saffron threads, dissolved in 50 ml (1¾ fl oz) hot water

400 g (14 oz) tinned chickpeas (garbanzo beans), drained and rinsed

2½ tablespoons runny honey

2 teaspoons orange-blossom water (optional)

2 tablespoons chopped pistachio nuts or toasted almonds

FROM THE GREENGROCER

2 large onions, roughly chopped

4 garlic cloves, finely chopped

2 tablespoons roughly chopped flat-leaf (Italian) parsley or mint

2 tablespoons roughly chopped coriander (cilantro) leaves

a good squeeze of lemon (optional)

FROM THE BUTCHER

1.5 kg (3 lb 5 oz) boneless lamb shoulder, cut into large chunks

Heat the olive oil and the butter in a large heavy-based saucepan over a high heat and brown the lamb on all sides, working in batches. Remove the meat from the pan as it browns and set aside.

Add the onions to the pan and stir well in the meat juices. Cook over a low heat until the onions have softened a little, then add the garlic, ginger, cinnamon and salt and pepper. Cook for 1 minute. Throw in the apricots, berries, stock and saffron in its water. Bring to the boil. Add the lamb plus any juices that have run out of it. Reduce the heat to very low and leave to cook, covered, for 1 hour 30 minutes–2 hours, stirring from time to time.

When the lamb has been cooking for 1 hour stir in the chickpeas. Cook for 30 minutes and then stir in the honey. Check to see whether the lamb needs further cooking – it needs to be completely tender. When the lamb is done, add the herbs, orange-blossom water (if using) and lemon juice (if using). Check for seasoning and flavour – you might want to add a little more honey. Sprinkle with the nuts and serve.

SERVES : 6   PREPARATION : 30 mins   COOKING : 30 mins

SEVEN VEGETABLE COUSCOUS
WITH MOROCCAN SPICES

Confusingly, couscous is both the name of a grain and the name of a dish that is simply served with the grain. This version is the most basic form of the latter, and you should adapt it according to whatever vegetables are in season.

FROM THE GROCER

80 ml (2½ fl oz/⅓ cup) olive oil

¾ teaspoon ground turmeric

2.25 litres (76 fl oz/9 cups) water or chicken stock

a good pinch of saffron threads

1 cinnamon stick

2 generous handfuls of raisins

salt and freshly ground black pepper

400 g (14 oz) tinned chickpeas (garbanzo beans), drained and rinsed

400 g (14 oz) couscous

1 tablespoon harissa, or to taste

FROM THE GREENGROCER

2 onions, cut into wedges

2.5 cm (1 in) piece fresh ginger, peeled and chopped

3 garlic cloves, finely chopped

1 small butternut pumpkin (squash), about 500 g (1 lb 2 oz), seeded and cut into chunks

3 potatoes, peeled and cut into 1 cm (½ in) slices

3 large carrots, cut into big chunks

2 small fennel bulbs, outer leaves removed, trimmed and quartered, fronds reserved

4 zucchini (courgettes), cut into thick slices

3 tomatoes, quartered

a medium bunch of coriander (cilantro), leaves removed and roughly chopped, stalks chopped

Heat 2 tablespoons of the olive oil in a large saucepan over a medium heat and cook the onions until soft and starting to colour. Reduce the heat. Add the ginger, garlic and turmeric and cook for another 2 minutes. Add the pumpkin, potatoes, carrots and 1.5 litres (51 fl oz/ 6 cups) of the water or stock. When hot, crumble in the saffron threads and add the cinnamon stick and raisins. Season with salt and pepper, bring to the boil, reduce the heat to medium and cover.

Remove the core from each fennel quarter. Once the vegetables have cooked for 10 minutes add the fennel, zucchini, tomatoes and coriander stalks. Cook for a further 15 minutes, stirring from time to time, until the vegetables are completely soft. Add the chickpeas 5 minutes before the end of cooking so they have time to heat through.

About 10 minutes before serving, put the couscous in a bowl, heat the remaining stock or water until boiling and pour over. Add the remaining oil, season well and mix. Cover with plastic wrap and set aside until the liquid has been absorbed, about 10 minutes. Using a fork, fluff up the couscous to aerate and separate the grains

When the vegetables are ready, remove a large ladleful of broth from the pan and mix with the harissa in a small pot and have it on the table so people can help themselves. Add the chopped coriander leaves and the fennel fronds to the vegetables just before serving, with the couscous alongside.

BRAISED RABBIT
WITH BROAD BEANS, BACON & MINT

Instead of wild rabbit, you can make this with chicken joints or thighs, or with farmed rabbit. Just reduce the cooking time to 45 minutes if you do.

FROM THE GROCER

salt and freshly ground black pepper

15 g (½ oz) unsalted butter

40 ml (1¼ fl oz) olive oil

500 ml (17 fl oz/2 cups) chicken stock

FROM THE GREENGROCER

1 onion, finely chopped

2 garlic cloves, finely chopped

500 g (1 lb 2 oz) fresh broad (fava) beans (podded weight)

5 mint sprigs, leaves picked and torn

FROM THE BUTCHER

12 wild rabbit joints (rabbit pieces on the bone)

150 g (5½ oz) bacon, cut into chunks

Season the rabbit joints well with salt and pepper. Heat the butter and half of the olive oil in a sauté pan over a high heat, add the rabbit and brown well. Remove the rabbit from the pan and set aside. Add the onion and sauté over a medium heat until soft and pale gold. Add the garlic and cook for another 2 minutes.

Return the rabbit to the pan, then add the stock. Bring to the boil, reduce the heat to very low, cover and gently cook the rabbit until it is tender, about 1 hour 40 minutes. Make sure the rabbit stays moist during this time and add a little more water or stock if you need to. Meanwhile, cook the beans in boiling salted water until tender, then drain. When cool enough to handle, slip off the skins and set aside.

Once the rabbit is cooked, remove from the pan with a slotted spoon and reduce the cooking liquid if you need to – you should have enough to just coat the rabbit. Heat the remaining oil in a frying pan and fry the bacon until golden. Add the beans, bacon and rabbit to the pan with the reduced cooking liquid. Heat through and check the seasoning. Add the mint leaves and serve.

This is good with plain, boiled waxy potatoes or a rice pilaff.

BRAISED BRETON LAMB
WITH TOMATOES, HARICOT BEANS & ROSEMARY

This old-fashioned and comforting dish is also lovely with pumpkin (winter squash) instead of carrot. A little Italian touch – a sprinkling of finely chopped parsley mixed with lemon zest and a couple of garlic cloves added at the end – is good too.

FROM THE GROCER

250 g (9 oz/1¼ cups) dried haricot (navy) beans, soaked overnight and drained

2 dried bay leaves

1 tablespoon olive oil

400 ml (13½ fl oz) lamb stock or water

400 g (14 oz) tinned chopped tomatoes

salt and freshly ground black pepper

FROM THE GREENGROCER

2 onions, peeled

8 flat-leaf (Italian) parsley stalks, plus 2 tablespoons chopped parsley

4 garlic cloves

1 celery stalk, diced

1 large carrot, diced

2 rosemary sprigs

FROM THE BUTCHER

800 g (1 lb 12 oz) lamb shoulder, excess fat removed, cubed

Put the beans into a saucepan and cover with water. Cut 1 of the onions into quarters and add to the pan with the bay leaves, parsley stalks and garlic. Bring to the boil, reduce the heat and simmer for 45 minutes. Drain and reserve the cooking liquor.

While the beans are cooking, roughly chop the remaining onion. Heat the olive oil in a heavy-based flameproof casserole over a high heat and brown the lamb in batches, making sure each piece is coloured all over. As each batch is cooked, remove and set aside. Add the chopped onion to the casserole dish with the celery and carrot and cook until well coloured.

Return the lamb to the dish and add all the remaining ingredients except the beans. Bring to the boil, reduce the heat to very low and cover. The lamb needs to gently simmer for a total of 2 hours, but 45 minutes before the end of cooking, add the beans. The lamb should be quite wet at this stage, but add some of the reserved cooking liquor if you feel it is too dry. If the lamb is very wet once you have added the beans, cook uncovered for a while. Continue to cook until the lamb has had its full 2 hours of gentle simmering. Towards the end of cooking, season really well with salt and pepper. The beans should be soft and the lamb tender.

GREEK VEGETABLE STIFADO

You can use beans you have cooked yourself for this but using tinned beans means you can have a very hearty stew on the table in about 45 minutes.

FROM THE GROCER

60 ml (2 fl oz/¼ cup) olive oil

¼ teaspoon ground cloves

½ cinnamon stick

80 ml (2½ fl oz/⅓ cup) tomato passata (puréed tomatoes)

1 tablespoon white wine vinegar

250 ml (8½ fl oz/1 cup) white wine

500 ml (17 fl oz/2 cups) chicken stock or water

2 dried bay leaves

1½ teaspoons soft light brown sugar

400 g (14 oz) tinned butterbeans or other white beans, drained and rinsed

salt and freshly ground black pepper

extra-virgin olive oil, for drizzling

FROM THE GREENGROCER

2 celery stalks, diced

2 small carrots, diced

250 g (9 oz) shallots or baby onions

350 g (12½ oz) leeks, white part only, washed, cut into 2 cm (¾ in) rounds

900 g (2 lb) butternut pumpkin (squash), peeled, seeded and cut into 2.5 cm (1 in) cubes

3 garlic cloves, chopped

4 oregano sprigs, plus extra leaves for garnish (optional)

Heat the olive oil in a flameproof casserole dish over a medium heat and sauté the celery, carrots and shallots or onions until soft and golden. Add the leeks and cook until starting to soften – about 4 minutes. Stir in the pumpkin, garlic, ground cloves and cinnamon stick and cook for about 2 minutes to release the flavour of the spices. Add everything else except the beans, salt and pepper, and extra-virgin olive oil. Stir. Bring to the boil, reduce the heat and cook for 15 minutes with the lid on. Add the beans and cook for a further 10 minutes, or until the squash is completely soft and the juices just coat all the vegetables. Taste for seasoning.

Remove the oregano sprigs from the dish and drizzle with extra-virgin olive oil. Serve with burghul (bulgur wheat) or brown rice and garnish with extra oregano leaves if you like.

pilaffs, risottos & paellas

BARLEY, SMOKED BACON & LEEK RISOTTO

Barley makes a good risotto because it becomes creamy and starchy as you stir it. You can use this recipe as a blueprint and make many of the risottos in your repertoire with barley instead of risotto rice.

FROM THE GROCER

50 g (1¾ oz) butter

1 tablespoon olive oil

1 litre (34 fl oz/4 cups) chicken stock

440 g (15½ oz/2 cups) pearl barley

salt and freshly ground black pepper

25 g (1 oz) grated parmesan, plus extra to serve

FROM THE GREENGROCER

3 leeks, white part only, washed and thinly sliced

4 tablespoons roughly chopped flat-leaf (Italian) parsley

FROM THE BUTCHER

150 g (5½ oz) smoked bacon, cut into lardons

Heat the butter and olive oil in a saucepan over a medium heat and fry the bacon until golden. Add the leeks, reduce the heat and gently sauté until soft but not coloured. In a separate saucepan, heat the stock and let it simmer gently. Stir the barley into the leeks, ensuring the grains are well coated in the buttery juices. Season with salt and pepper.

Add the stock to the barley pan one ladleful at a time, just as you do when making traditional risotto. Don't add the next ladleful of stock until the previous one has been absorbed. Eventually the barley will soften and become creamy, between 30 and 40 minutes. Add the parsley in the last 5 minutes of cooking.

Spoon the risotto into serving bowls and sprinkle 1 tablespoon parmesan over each. Put extra parmesan on the table for guests to help themselves.

PUMPKIN, CHESTNUT & FARRO RISOTTO

Risotto made with farro has a different texture from regular risotto – it is still a little creamy but has a deeper, nuttier flavour. It works particularly well with autumnal and wintry ingredients like pumpkin (winter squash) and chestnuts, and makes a good side dish for roast pork.

FROM THE GROCER
2 tablespoons olive oil
85 g (3 oz) butter
300 g (10½ oz) farro
salt and freshly ground black pepper
1 litre (34 fl oz/4 cups) chicken or vegetable stock
75 g (2¾ oz) cooked chestnuts, frozen or vacuum-packed
grated parmesan, to serve

FROM THE GREENGROCER
800 g (1 lb 12 oz) pumpkin (winter squash), peeled, seeded and cut into chunks
1 small onion, very finely chopped
2 garlic cloves, very finely chopped
1 celery stalk, very finely chopped
16 sage leaves

Heat the olive oil in a saucepan over a medium–high heat and cook the pumpkin in batches until the outside is slightly caramelised in patches – you just want to colour the pumpkin, not cook it through. Remove with a slotted spoon and set aside. In the same pan, melt 20 g (¾ oz) of the butter and add the onion, garlic and celery. Cook over a low heat until the onion is soft and translucent. Add the farro and stir, making sure the grains are well coated. Stir in the pumpkin. Season lightly with salt and pepper, and cover with the stock. Cook for about 35 minutes. Put the lid on for the first half of cooking, then continue uncovered. Unlike traditional risotto, you only need to stir this dish occasionally, but you will still end up with a mixture that is creamy like risotto. Taste for seasoning.

While the risotto is cooking, melt 30 g (1 oz) of the butter in a small frying pan over a medium heat and quickly fry the chestnuts until glossy and warm. Gently stir the chestnuts and their frying butter into the risotto, cover and remove from the heat.

Quickly fry the sage leaves in the remaining butter until crisp.

Spoon the risotto into soup bowls and top with the sage leaves. Drizzle over the sage frying butter, grind over some black pepper and top with parmesan. Serve immediately.

CAULIFLOWER RISOTTO
WITH GORGONZOLA & WALNUT GREMOLATA

This is a rich and delicious risotto that makes terrific use of cauliflower, an often underrated vegetable. The gorgonzola makes it wonderfully cheesy and packs a real flavour punch.

FROM THE GROCER

45 g (1½ oz) butter

300 g (10½ oz) brown risotto rice

150 ml (5 fl oz) dry white wine or dry vermouth

2 litres (68 fl oz/8 cups) hot chicken or vegetable stock

25 g (1 oz/¼ cup) walnuts, lightly toasted

crumbled gorgonzola, to serve

FROM THE GREENGROCER

1 small onion, finely chopped

1 cauliflower, about 400 g (14 oz), cut into florets

grated zest of 1 lemon, plus extra finely sliced zest for garnishing (optional)

2 garlic cloves

2 tablespoons chopped flat-leaf (Italian) parsley

Preheat the oven to 180°C (350°F). Melt 25 g (1 oz) of the butter in a small heavy-based ovenproof saucepan over a low–medium heat and sauté the onion until soft but not coloured. Add the rice and cook for about 3 minutes, stirring to coat well. Add the alcohol and let it simmer until there is almost none left, stirring constantly. Start adding the stock, one ladleful at a time, only adding the next ladleful when the previous one has been absorbed. Do this for 10 minutes, stirring constantly and then add half the remaining stock. Transfer the pan to the oven and cook for 30 minutes, then stir the rice well and add the rest of the stock – it must be hot. Continue cooking for another 20 minutes.

Meanwhile, boil or steam the cauliflower until just tender. Drain if needed. Heat the remaining butter in a frying pan over a medium–high heat and briskly sauté the cauliflower until golden and toasted in patches.

Make the gremolata by chopping together the lemon zest, garlic, parsley and walnuts.

At the end of its cooking time the rice should be creamy and quite soft, although still have a little bite. If the liquid has not been completely absorbed, cook a little longer over a medium heat, stirring. Stir most of the cauliflower into the risotto, reserving some to scatter on top at the end.

Serve in shallow soup bowls with the reserved cauliflower on top and the gremolata, gorgonzola and sliced lemon zest (if using) scattered over.

BEETROOT RISOTTO
WITH GOAT'S CHEESE & WATERCRESS PESTO

This risotto is an amazing colour. If you don't want to make the pesto just serve the risotto scattered with the goat's cheese and perhaps some chopped parsley or little pea shoots.

FROM THE GROCER

30 g (1 oz) butter

2 tablespoons olive oil

2 litres (68 fl oz/8 cups) chicken or vegetable stock

300 g (10½ oz) brown risotto rice

125 ml (4 fl oz/½ cup) dry vermouth

25 g (1 oz) blanched almonds

25 g (1 oz) lightly toasted walnut pieces

75 g (2¾ oz) hard goat's cheese, grated

150 ml (5 fl oz) fruity extra-virgin olive oil

80 ml (2½ fl oz) thick (double/heavy) cream

salt and freshly ground black pepper

110 g (4 oz) soft goat's cheese, crumbled

FROM THE GREENGROCER

400 g (14 oz) beetroot (beets), grated

4 shallots, finely chopped

3 garlic cloves, finely chopped

65 g (2¼ oz) watercress

a squeeze of lemon juice

Preheat the oven to 180°C (350°F). Heat the butter and olive oil in a heavy-based ovenproof saucepan over a medium heat. Add the beetroot, shallots and two-thirds of the garlic. Cook gently for 5 minutes, or until the shallots have softened but not coloured. In a separate saucepan, heat the stock to simmering point.

Add the rice to the beetroot mixture and stir to coat in the buttery juices. Cook, stirring, for 1–2 minutes, or until the grains begin to look translucent. Add the vermouth and allow it to bubble up and reduce slightly. Add one small ladleful of the simmering stock and stir until all of the liquid has been absorbed. Continue adding the stock one ladleful at a time for 10 minutes, then add half of the remaining stock. Transfer the pan to the oven and cook for 30 minutes. Remove the pan and stir the rice well. Add the rest of the stock – it must be hot – and return the pan to the oven for a further 20–25 minutes, or until the rice is creamy and soft and the liquid has been absorbed. If it is still soupy after this time, stir over a medium heat on the stovetop until the liquid has been absorbed.

To make the pesto, place the watercress, almonds, walnuts, hard goat's cheese, extra-virgin olive oil and the remaining garlic in a food processor and process. Scrape into a bowl and stir in the cream and squeeze of lemon juice.

When the risotto is cooked, taste for seasoning. Serve with some of the pesto drizzled on top of each serving, and scatter with the crumbled soft goat's cheese.

LEEK & SMOKED HADDOCK RISOTTO

This is a very simple, homely risotto but you can make it more chic and substantial by serving it with a poached egg on top or a dollop of crème fraîche into which you've mixed finely chopped soft herbs, freshly grated horseradish or wholegrain mustard.

FROM THE GROCER

45 g (1½ oz) butter

300 g (10½ oz) brown risotto rice

150 ml (5 fl oz) dry white wine or dry vermouth

2.5 litres (85 fl oz/10 cups) hot chicken or vegetable stock

60 g (2 oz) grated parmesan, plus extra to serve

salt and freshly ground black pepper

FROM THE GREENGROCER

4 leeks, white part only, thinly sliced

FROM THE FISHMONGER

450 g (1 lb) smoked haddock

Preheat the oven to 180°C (350°F). Melt the butter in a heavy-based ovenproof saucepan over a medium heat and add the leeks. Add a couple of tablespoons of water, stir well, reduce the heat to low and cover. Leave to sweat for about 10 minutes so that the leeks become nice and soft. Add the rice and cook for about 3 minutes, making sure it is well coated in the buttery juices. Pour in the alcohol and simmer until there is almost none left, stirring all the time.

Set aside 500 ml (17 fl oz/2 cups) of the stock for poaching the fish. Start adding the remaining stock to the rice, one small ladleful at a time, only adding the next ladleful when the previous one has been absorbed. The amount you add at this stage shouldn't exceed 250 ml (9 fl oz/1 cup). Cook, stirring, for 10 minutes and then add half of the remaining risotto stock. Transfer the pan to the oven, cook for 30 minutes and then stir the rice well. Add the rest of the risotto stock – it must be hot – and return the pan to the oven for a further 20–25 minutes, or until the rice is creamy and soft and the liquid has been absorbed. If it is still soupy after this time, stir over a medium heat on the stovetop until the liquid has been absorbed.

Pour the reserved stock into a sauté pan and bring to the boil. Reduce the heat to a very gentle simmer and poach the fish for about 5 minutes. Transfer the fish to a plate, remove the skin and gently flake the flesh into chunky pieces. Once the risotto is cooked, carefully stir in the fish and the parmesan. Add black pepper and taste for seasoning – the fish is quite salty so you probably won't need any salt. Serve the risotto with the remaining parmesan on the side.

QUINOA, CHICKEN & BLACK BEANS
WITH AVOCADO PURÉE

Make this as hot as you like by adding more chilli. It has many of the elements of a chilli con carne, but in a rather more healthy form.

FROM THE GROCER

80 ml (2½ fl oz/⅓ cup) extra-virgin olive oil

1 tablespoon sherry vinegar

300 g (10½ oz/1½ cups) quinoa

75 ml (2½ fl oz) peanut or sunflower oil

salt and freshly ground black pepper

675 ml (23 fl oz) chicken or vegetable stock, or water

1 teaspoon ground cumin

½ teaspoon ground turmeric

400 g (14 oz) tinned black (turtle) beans, drained and rinsed

sour cream, to serve

crumbled feta cheese, to serve (optional)

FROM THE GREENGROCER

2 avocados

5 garlic cloves

60 ml (2 fl oz/¼ cup) lime juice, plus lime wedges, to serve

1 small bunch of coriander (cilantro), leaves picked and chopped

1 small red or white onion, finely chopped, plus 1 red onion, thinly sliced

2 red capsicums (bell peppers), halved, seeded and cut into strips

1 red chilli, halved, seeded and cut into slivers

8 spring onions (scallions), chopped

FROM THE BUTCHER

350 g (12½ oz) boneless, skinless chicken breast, cut into strips

To make the purée, place the avocado flesh, 2 of the garlic cloves, the extra-virgin olive oil, 2 tablespoons of the lime juice, the sherry vinegar and 2 tablespoons of the coriander in a food processor. Process until smooth and set aside.

Toast the quinoa in a dry frying pan over a medium heat for 3 minutes. It should darken a little, smell slightly toasted and start to pop. Remove from the heat and set aside.

Heat 2 tablespoons of the peanut or sunflower oil in a saucepan over a medium heat and add the small chopped onion. Cook until soft and slightly golden. Finely chop the remaining garlic and add to the pan. Cook for 2 minutes, stir through the quinoa and season with salt and pepper. Cover with the stock, stir and bring to the boil. Immediately reduce the heat to very low, cover and cook for 15–20 minutes, or until the liquid has been absorbed.

Meanwhile, heat the remaining peanut or sunflower oil in a frying pan and cook the capsicum until soft. Add the red onion and cook until it is soft too. Add the chicken, cumin, chilli and turmeric and fry until the chicken is cooked through and the capsicum is slightly singed at the edges. Add the black beans and spring onions, then season. Cook until the beans are warmed through.

Gently toss the quinoa through the chicken mixture and add the remaining coriander. Pour over the rest of the lime juice and check the seasoning. Serve with the avocado purée, sour cream and lime wedges. Crumble the feta on top (if using) – it isn't the same as the Mexican cheese *queso fresco*, but it's not a bad substitute.

MIDDLE EASTERN PILAFF
WITH TZATZIKI

This is very autumnal and perfect as a side dish for spicy roast chicken or lamb.

FROM THE GROCER

125 g (4½ oz/⅔ cup) brown lentils

60 ml (2 fl oz/¼ cup) olive oil

1½ teaspoons cumin

2 teaspoons cayenne pepper

200 g (7 oz) burghul (bulgur wheat)

375 ml (12½ fl oz/1½ cups) chicken or vegetable stock

salt and freshly ground black pepper

12 pitted dates, chopped

350 g (12½ oz) Greek-style yoghurt

2 tablespoons extra-virgin olive oil

25 g (1 oz/¼ cup) flaked almonds, toasted

1 tablespoon toasted white sesame seeds, for sprinkling

FROM THE GREENGROCER

1 onion, chopped

4 garlic cloves

1 Lebanese (short) cucumber, peeled, seeded and cut into small cubes

2 tablespoons roughly chopped mint

juice of ½ lemon

15 g (½ oz/¼ cup) chopped coriander (cilantro)

Put the lentils in a saucepan and cover with water. Bring to the boil, reduce the heat and cook until soft but not falling apart, about 20–35 minutes.

Meanwhile, in a separate saucepan, sauté the onion in 1 tablespoon of the olive oil until soft but not coloured. Add 2 of the garlic cloves (finely chopped), the cumin and cayenne pepper and cook for another 2 minutes. Stir in the burghul, stock, seasoning and dates. Bring to the boil, reduce the heat to a very gentle simmer, cover and cook until the liquid has been absorbed and the burghul is cooked, about 15 minutes.

Make the tzatziki by combining the yoghurt with the remaining garlic (crushed), the remaining olive oil, the cucumber and mint. Stir gently to avoid squashing the cucumber.

Drain the lentils, season with salt and pepper and stir in the extra-virgin olive oil and lemon juice. Carefully fork the lentils through the burghul, along with the coriander and almonds. Check for seasoning. Sprinkle with the sesame seeds and serve with the tzatziki.

THIS delicious seasoning is a healthy alternative to pure salt and has a punchier flavour thanks to the toasted sesame seeds. Gomashio is widely used in Japan to sprinkle over plain rice and is also very good with steamed vegetables or tofu.

how to
MAKE GOMASHIO

1 Put 35 g (1 ¼ oz/¼ cup) sea salt flakes into a dry frying pan and toast, gently stirring all the time, until they turn grey. Transfer to a plate to cool.

2 Toast 500 g (1 lb 2 oz) white sesame seeds in the same way, stirring frequently, until they turn a shade darker. Be careful not to burn them.

3 Put the salt and the seeds into a clean spice mill, food processor or mortar.

4 Grind the salt and seeds, using the pulse button if using a machine, until you have a coarse powder. Don't overwork or the seeds will break down and become oily.

Gomasio

5 Tip the mixture into a large jar, label and seal.

6 Keep somewhere dry and use within 2 months.

ROAST DUCK BREAST
WITH HERBED FREEKEH & PRESERVED LEMON

Freekeh has a really assertive taste – the smell is like wet straw as it cooks – but try it once and you will be addicted. It goes best with strong ingredients like duck, lamb, game, dried fruits, preserved lemons and capers.

FROM THE GROCER

200 g (7 oz) freekeh

1 teaspoon salt

freshly ground black pepper

2 tablespoons olive oil

1 tablespoon peanut oil

50 g (1¾ oz) ready-to-eat dried figs, chopped

125 ml (4 fl oz/½ cup) extra-virgin olive oil

FROM THE GREENGROCER

rind from 2 small preserved lemons, cut into tiny dice

a generous handful each of mint and flat-leaf (Italian) parsley, chopped

juice of 1½ lemons

FROM THE BUTCHER

4 boneless duck breasts, skin scored

Put the freekeh into a saucepan with 1.25 litres (42 fl oz/5 cups) water, the salt and olive oil. Bring to the boil. Cover with a tight-fitting lid, reduce the heat and simmer for 25–30 minutes. The water should be absorbed during cooking and the grains should become tender. Drain any remaining water. Remove from the heat and set aside.

Preheat the oven to 220°C (430°F). Season the duck breasts and heat a frying pan until very hot. Fry the duck, skin side down, in the peanut oil until golden. Turn the breasts over and cook until coloured – this should only take a couple of minutes. Put the duck in a roasting tin and roast for 7–9 minutes. As you are going to slice the duck breasts anyway you can make a slit in one to check if they are ready – you want them rare. When cooked, remove to a plate, cover with foil, insulate with a number of tea towels (dish towels) – I use 4 – and leave to rest for about 10 minutes.

Toss the lemon rind with the freekeh, along with the figs, herbs, lemon juice and extra-virgin olive oil. Season with pepper – you shouldn't need salt, as the preserved lemon is salty, but check to see.

Slice the duck breast neatly and toss with the freekeh. Serve with a small fresh watercress salad, or other green salad.

SPANISH SAFFRON RICE
WITH CHICKEN, CHORIZO & PEAS

This is based on regular Spanish paella, which is normally made using special paella rice. This is less creamy but produces a very good dish, as brown rice works particularly well with the big flavours of chorizo and smoked paprika. It's essential to use a broad and shallow pan.

FROM THE GROCER

80 ml (2½ fl oz/⅓ cup) olive oil

salt and freshly ground black pepper

1¼ tablespoons smoked paprika

a good pinch of saffron threads

1 litre (34 fl oz/4 cups) hot chicken stock

350 g (12½ oz) brown risotto rice

extra-virgin olive oil, for drizzling

FROM THE GREENGROCER

1 red capsicum (bell pepper), halved, seeded and sliced

1 green capsicum, halved, seeded and sliced

1 large onion, roughly chopped

4 garlic cloves, crushed

150 g (5½ oz) fresh or frozen peas (podded weight)

1 tablespoon chopped flat-leaf (Italian) parsley

juice of ½ lemon

FROM THE BUTCHER

6 large chicken thighs on the bone, skin on

250 g (9 oz) chorizo, cut into small chunks

Heat the olive oil in a broad and shallow heavy-based frying pan over a high heat. Season the chicken and brown all over. Remove the chicken from the pan and set aside. Reduce the heat to medium, add the capsicum and chorizo and sauté until the capsicum begins to soften. Add the onion and garlic and cook gently until the onion is soft. Sprinkle in the paprika and cook for 1 minute, stirring.

Dissolve the saffron in the stock and pour into the pan with the capsicum and chorizo. Add the rice, bring to the boil, then reduce the heat and simmer with the lid on for 20 minutes. Return the chicken pieces to the pan – just set them on top of the rice, skin side up – and season well. Simmer uncovered for another 40 minutes.

About 5 minutes before the end of cooking, boil the peas in salted water until tender and then drain. Gently mix the peas into the chicken and rice. When the cooking time is up all the stock should have been absorbed (add a little more if it seems to be getting too dry) and the chicken cooked through.

Scatter with the parsley, squeeze the lemon juice over the top and drizzle with a little extra-virgin olive oil just before serving.

SPANISH RICE
WITH PORK, BROAD BEANS, SPINACH & MINT

This proves it's possible to make a paella-style dish with brown risotto rice – it just takes a little longer to cook than traditional Spanish rice but pays you back for the extra effort by delivering a really deep flavour.

FROM THE GROCER

salt and freshly ground black pepper

105 ml (3½ fl oz) olive oil

¼ teaspoon dried chilli flakes

250 g (9 oz) brown risotto rice

1.2 litres (41 fl oz) hot chicken stock or water

extra-virgin olive oil, for drizzling

FROM THE GREENGROCER

2 large onions, roughly chopped

2 red capsicums (bell peppers), halved, seeded and sliced

4 garlic cloves, finely chopped

650 g (1 lb 7 oz) English spinach, tough stalks removed

125 g (4½ oz) broad (fava) beans (podded weight)

a handful of mint leaves, torn

juice of ½ lemon

FROM THE BUTCHER

350 g (12½ oz) pork fillet, cut in half lengthways and sliced

300 g (10½ oz) piece streaky bacon, cut into chunks

Season the pork with salt and pepper. Heat 2 tablespoons of the olive oil in a large shallow saucepan or frying pan over a high heat and quickly brown the meat on all sides. Remove the pork from the pan and set aside. Reduce the heat and add another 2 tablespoons of the oil. Sauté the bacon for a couple of minutes and add the onions and capsicums. Cook over a medium–low heat for 20 minutes, or until the vegetables are soft. Add the garlic and chilli flakes and cook for another couple of minutes, then add the rice. Stir to coat in the juices, pour over the stock and season with salt and pepper. Bring to the boil, reduce the heat to very low and cover. Cook for 1 hour.

Meanwhile, heat the remaining oil in a frying pan over a medium heat and wilt the spinach. When cooked, chop the spinach and season. Cook the broad beans in lightly salted boiling water until tender. Drain and reserve the cooking water. Slip the skins off the beans.

About 5 minutes before the end of cooking, distribute the spinach over the top of the rice and tuck in the pieces of pork. Check for seasoning, reduce the heat to very low and cover while it cooks for the final 5 minutes. Gently fork through the drained broad beans and the mint. Squeeze the lemon juice over the top, drizzle with extra-virgin olive oil and serve immediately.

KUSHARY

This is delicious served with Greek-style yoghurt and the spicy tomato sauce on page 194. Just add a seeded and chopped chilli to the sauce to give it a little kick and, ideally, purée it before you serve it with this dish.

FROM THE GROCER

70 g (2½ oz) brown lentils

50 g (1¾ oz/¼ cup) long-grain white rice

90 ml (3 fl oz) olive oil

50 g (1¾ oz/⅓ cup) small macaroni

salt and freshly ground black pepper

½ teaspoon ground cumin

200 ml (7 fl oz) chicken, meat or vegetable stock, or water

FROM THE GREENGROCER

2 onions, roughly chopped

Rinse the lentils and soak them in cold water for 30 minutes. Rinse the rice until the water runs clear, then leave to soak for 30 minutes. Drain.

Heat 60 ml (2 fl oz/¼ cup) of the olive oil in a frying pan over a medium–low heat and sauté the onions until browned and starting to caramelise. This should take about 15 minutes. You'll need to keep an eye on the pan and stir from time to time, as you don't want them to burn. Remove from the heat and set aside.

Cook the macaroni in lightly salted boiling water until al dente, then drain. Heat 1 tablespoon of the oil in a frying pan over a medium heat and sauté the cooked pasta until it starts to colour at the edges. Set aside.

Heat the remaining oil in a heavy-based saucepan over a medium heat. Stir the lentils and rice around in the oil and add the cumin. Cook for about 1 minute, then add the stock and season with salt and pepper.

Let the rice and lentils simmer uncovered for about 25 minutes, then stir in the macaroni. Cover and cook undisturbed over a low heat for 5 minutes, or until the base of the pan is browned. Stir to break up the crispy bits. Add the onions and mix everything together. Check the seasoning and serve.

LAMB & BURGHUL PILAFF
WITH APRICOTS, PRESERVED LEMON & PISTACHIOS

This recipe is good for using up left-over roast lamb – just cut it into chunks. It also works particularly well with chicken.

FROM THE GROCER

2 tablespoons olive oil, plus extra for frying

½ teaspoon ground allspice

175 g (6 oz/1 cup) burghul (bulgur wheat)

350 ml (12 fl oz) chicken or lamb stock

salt and freshly ground black pepper

50 g (1¾ oz) dried apricots, chopped

35 g (1¼ oz/¼ cup) unsalted pistachio nuts, shelled

rind of 1 preserved lemon, shredded

FROM THE GREENGROCER

1 onion, roughly chopped

1 red chilli, halved, seeded and thinly sliced

2 garlic cloves, crushed

2 tablespoons chopped flat-leaf (Italian) parsley or mint, or a mixture of both

FROM THE BUTCHER

500 g (1 lb 2 oz) lamb fillet, cut into chunks

Heat the olive oil in a sauté pan over a medium heat and cook the lamb until it has a good colour all over and is cooked but still rare. Lift out with a slotted spoon and set aside.

In the same pan, cook the onion until soft and golden – you might need to add a little more oil. Stir in the chilli, allspice and garlic and sauté for 1 minute. Add the burghul and stir briefly to coat. Add the stock, salt and pepper, and apricots. Bring to the boil and immediately reduce the heat to low. Cover and cook for 15 minutes, or until the liquid has been absorbed and the burghul is tender.

Season and gently fork through the cooked lamb. Cover the pan, remove from the heat and leave to stand for a further 15 minutes to let the burghul fluff up. Gently fork through the pistachio nuts, herbs and preserved lemon rind. Plain Greek-style yoghurt is good on the side.

dinner

BRETON TUNA & BEAN GRATIN

You can whip up this great pantry dish on a Sunday evening when there is very little to eat in the house. Despite containing such a large quantity of beans this is not a dry dish, but rich and comforting.

FROM THE GROCER

1½ teaspoons olive oil

800 g (1 lb 12 oz) tinned haricot (navy) beans

salt and freshly ground black pepper

2 tablespoons thick (double/heavy) cream

2 tablespoons milk

185 g (6½ oz) tinned tuna in olive oil

1 small dried red chilli, crumbled (optional)

40 g (1½ oz/⅓ cup) grated gruyère

2 tablespoons coarse white breadcrumbs

15 g (½ oz) butter

FROM THE GREENGROCER

1 onion, finely chopped

6 garlic cloves, thinly sliced

1½ teaspoons chopped flat-leaf (Italian) parsley

Preheat the oven to 180°C (350°F). Heat the olive oil in a frying pan over a low–medium heat and sauté the onion until soft but not coloured. Add the garlic and cook for another 4 minutes or so. Drain half the tinned beans and add to the pan, then add the remaining tinned beans and their juices. Season well with salt and pepper and set the pan over a low heat so that the beans can meld with the onion.

Transfer the beans and onion to a food processor and blitz to a purée. Add the cream and milk and mix these in too. Tip the mixture into a bowl and add the tuna and its olive oil, the chilli (if using) and half the gruyère. Stir together and taste for seasoning. Scrape the mixture into a small gratin dish and sprinkle the breadcrumbs and the rest of the gruyère on top. Dot little nuggets of the butter all over the breadcrumbs and bake for 20 minutes, sprinkling the parsley over 5 minutes before the end of cooking. Serve with a green vegetable such as broccoli.

BREAM FILLETS
WITH WHITE BEAN PURÉE & BURGHUL

This dish is a lovely mixture of strong and subtle flavours – powerfully flavoured olives, anchovies and capers with a plain bean purée. Be careful not to add too much liquid to the burghul.

FROM THE GROCER

120 ml (4 fl oz) olive oil

800 g (1 lb 12 oz) tinned cannellini (lima) beans, drained

150 ml (5 fl oz) light chicken stock or water

salt and freshly ground black pepper

180 ml (6 fl oz) extra-virgin olive oil, plus extra for drizzling

50 g (1¾ oz) tinned anchovies, drained and chopped

2 tablespoons capers, rinsed

2 teaspoons white balsamic vinegar

100 g (3½ oz) burghul (bulgur wheat)

200 ml (7 fl oz) chicken or vegetable stock or water

75 g (2¾ oz) pitted black olives, chopped

seasoned plain (all-purpose) flour

FROM THE GREENGROCER

½ white onion, roughly chopped

5 garlic cloves

2 tablespoons lemon juice, plus lemon wedges, to serve

1 fennel bulb, trimmed, quartered and cored

2 tablespoons chopped mint

1 red onion, finely chopped

1½ tablespoons very finely chopped flat-leaf (Italian) parsley

FROM THE FISHMONGER

700–800 g (1 lb 9 oz–1 lb 12 oz) bream fillets

Heat 2 tablespoons of the olive oil in a saucepan over a low–medium heat and cook the white onion until soft but not coloured. Add 1 of the garlic cloves (crushed), the beans, the light chicken stock and salt and pepper. Cook over a medium heat for about 4 minutes. Process the beans and the cooking liquid in a blender with 80 ml (2½ fl oz/⅓ cup) of the extra-virgin olive oil and 1 tablespoon of the lemon juice. Taste for seasoning.

For the relish, dice the fennel and fry in 2 tablespoons of the olive oil over a medium heat until just softening. Add 2 of the garlic cloves (chopped) and cook for 1 minute. Transfer to a bowl and add the anchovies, mint, capers, vinegar, pepper and 90 ml (3 fl oz) of the extra-virgin olive oil. Stir and taste for seasoning. Set aside.

Sauté the red onion in 1 tablespoon of the olive oil in a saucepan over a medium heat. When soft and translucent add the remaining garlic (crushed) and cook for another couple of minutes. Add the burghul, then pour over the chicken or vegetable stock and season. Bring to the boil, reduce the heat and simmer for 15 minutes, or until all the stock has been absorbed. Ensure the burghul doesn't catch on the bottom of the pan. Remove from the heat, cover and set aside for 10 minutes. Add the olives and fork through the burghul with the parsley, the remaining extra-virgin olive oil and the remaining lemon juice. Taste and adjust the seasoning.

Dip the fish fillets in the flour and shake off any excess. Heat the remaining olive oil in a frying pan and cook the fish, skin side down, over a medium heat for 3 minutes until brown. Carefully turn over and repeat.

Put a portion of the burghul onto each plate and spoon over some bean purée. Put the fish fillets on top and add the relish. Offer the remaining burghul and bean purée in serving bowls. Drizzle each serving with extra-virgin olive oil and serve with wedges of lemon.

MACKEREL & OAT FISHCAKES
WITH HORSERADISH MAYONNAISE

The oats here make a lovely crispy coating. If you prefer the dish to be slightly healthier, serve it with horseradish sauce rather than horseradish mayo.

FROM THE GROCER

15 g (½ oz) butter

2 small eggs

75 g (2¾ oz/½ cup) seasoned plain (all-purpose) flour, plus extra for dusting

175 g (6 oz) good-quality store-bought mayonnaise

3 tablespoons crème fraîche

100 g (3½ oz) pinhead oats or rolled (porridge) oats

80 ml (2½ fl oz/⅓ cup) peanut oil

FROM THE GREENGROCER

500 g (1 lb 2 oz) potatoes

1 small onion, finely chopped

2 tablespoons finely chopped flat-leaf (Italian) parsley

150 g (5½ oz) English spinach, washed, stalks removed

1 tablespoon grated fresh horseradish, or from a jar

lemon wedges, to serve

watercress, to serve (optional)

FROM THE FISHMONGER

275 g (9½ oz) smoked mackerel fillets

Boil the potatoes until tender. Remove and discard the skins, then mash the flesh. Remove and discard the skin from the fish and break the flesh into large flakes.

Sauté the onion in the butter in a frying pan over a low–medium heat until soft but not coloured and add the parsley. Remove from the heat and set aside.

Put the spinach into a saucepan with 1 tablespoon water, cover and cook for 90 seconds over a very low heat. Drain, squeeze out all the water and roughly chop. Set aside.

Mix together the mashed potato, the sautéed onion and the spinach. Carefully incorporate the fish and 1 of the eggs, being careful not to break up the fish too much. Flour your hands well and form the mixture into little cakes about 8 cm (3¼ in) across. Chill for 30 minutes. Meanwhile, stir together the mayonnaise, horseradish and crème fraîche. Set aside.

In three separate shallow dishes place the remaining egg (lightly beaten), the seasoned flour and the oats. Dip each fishcake in the flour, then the egg, then the oats. The fishcakes should be completely coated. Heat the peanut oil in a large frying pan over a medium heat and fry the fishcakes for about 3 minutes on each side, reducing the heat once they have a nice golden crust.

Serve with the mayonnaise, wedges of lemon and watercress (if using).

SEARED TUNA
WITH WARM BEANS & SALSA VERDE

You can extend and adapt this recipe by adding roasted cherry tomatoes or cooked but still-crisp green beans to the white bean mixture.

FROM THE GROCER

8 tinned anchovies in oil, drained

1½ teaspoons dijon mustard

1 tablespoon capers, rinsed

150 ml (5 fl oz) extra-virgin olive oil

80 ml (2½ fl oz/⅓ cup) olive oil, plus extra for brushing

800 g (1 lb 12 oz) tinned cannellini (lima) beans

salt and freshly ground black pepper

FROM THE GREENGROCER

1 small bunch flat-leaf (Italian) parsley, leaves picked, plus 1 tablespoon very finely chopped parsley, extra

10 basil leaves

15 mint leaves

2 garlic cloves

juice of ½ lemon, plus a good squeeze of lemon

1 red onion, thinly sliced

FROM THE FISHMONGER

500 g (1 lb 2 oz) tuna loin, cut from the tail end

Make the salsa verde by putting most of the parsley leaves (reserving some to garnish), the anchovies, basil, mint, mustard, capers and 1 of the garlic cloves into a food processor. Pulse and add the extra-virgin olive oil as you go. Add the juice of ½ lemon, or to taste.

For the beans, heat 2 tablespoons of the olive oil in a frying pan over a low–medium heat and sauté the onion gently until soft but not coloured. Add the remaining garlic (finely chopped) and cook for 2 minutes. Add the beans and the remaining olive oil. Season and let the beans heat through and absorb the cooking juices. Add a squeeze of lemon and the tablespoon of finely chopped parsley. Taste for seasoning.

Just before you want to serve, brush the tuna with olive oil and season. Heat a chargrill pan until very hot and sear the fish on both sides until cooked to your liking. Don't cook it all the way through.

Spoon the beans onto serving plates. Using a fine knife, cut the tuna into little medallions and place them on top of the beans. Spoon over some salsa verde, garnish with the remaining parsley leaves and serve.

SALMON & LEMON COUSCOUS
WITH BROAD BEAN PURÉE, PANCETTA & MINT

As well as being an incredibly healthy dish that contains both beans and grains, this is very light and summery. You can leave the mint oil out, although it does make a simple dish special.

FROM THE GROCER
185 ml (6 fl oz) olive oil

¾ teaspoon caster (superfine) sugar

1 teaspoon white wine vinegar

100 g (3½ oz) butter, melted

2 tablespoons thick (double/heavy) cream

salt and freshly ground black pepper

500 g (1 lb 2 oz) wholemeal (whole-wheat) couscous

500 ml (17 fl oz/2 cups) chicken stock or water

60 ml (2 fl oz/¼ cup) extra-virgin olive oil

FROM THE GREENGROCER
5 large mint sprigs, leaves picked, plus 25 g (1 oz) mint leaves, torn into small pieces

500 g (1 lb 2 oz) fresh or frozen broad (fava) beans (podded weight)

1 small onion, very finely chopped

juice of 4 lemons, plus a squeeze of lemon

zest of 3 lemons, sliced very thinly

FROM THE FISHMONGER
6 x 175 g (6 oz) salmon fillets

FROM THE BUTCHER
200 g (7 oz) unsmoked pancetta, cut into chunks

To make the mint oil, put 125 ml (4 fl oz/½ cup) of the olive oil, the leaves from the 5 mint sprigs, the sugar and vinegar in a blender and process. Taste to see if it has a good sweet–sour balance. Cover and set aside to let the flavours infuse.

For the purée, cook the beans in boiling water until tender and then drain. When cool enough to handle, slip off the skins and tip the beans into a blender or food processor. Add the butter, cream, salt and pepper and the squeeze of lemon. Blend until smooth and set aside.

Heat 1 tablespoon of the olive oil in a frying pan over a low–medium heat and sauté the onion until soft but not coloured and set aside. Put the couscous into a large bowl. Heat the stock or water to boiling then pour over the couscous and cover tightly with plastic wrap. Leave for 10 minutes to plump up.

Heat the remaining olive oil in two frying pans. Season the salmon and cook 3 fillets in each pan over a medium heat, flesh side down, for 1½–2 minutes, or until golden. Turn the fish over and repeat. Reduce the heat, cover the pan and let the salmon continue to cook until it is cooked through but still moist. In a separate frying pan over a medium heat, quickly sauté the pancetta in its own fat while the fish is cooking.

Warm the bean purée. Fluff up and aerate the couscous using a fork and add the onion and the lemon zest. Pour in the lemon juice gradually, tasting as you go, until the couscous is as lemony as you want it. Add the 25 g (1 oz) mint leaves and the extra-virgin olive oil. Flake the salmon into the couscous and add the pan juices and the pancetta. Toss gently and taste for seasoning.

Divide the salmon couscous between six plates and put a spoonful of the broad bean purée on top. Serve drizzled with the mint oil.

QUICK IDEAS
coatings

Mixed grain coating

Mix together 25 g (1 oz/¼ cup) each rolled (porridge) oats, wheat flakes and dry brown breadcrumbs. Season. Combine 1 beaten egg and 1 tablespoon milk in a soup bowl. Put 35 g (1¼ oz/¼ cup) wholemeal (whole-wheat) flour on a large plate. Dip fish fillets, flattened boneless, skinless chicken breasts or risotto cakes in the flour, then the egg mixture, then the mixed grains. Chill for 30 minutes before frying. Makes enough for 4 fillets or cakes.

Pinhead oats

Mix 100 g (3½ oz) pinhead oats with salt and freshly ground black pepper and spread on a large plate. Press whole fish, such as herring or mackerel, into the oatmeal on both sides then fry in a mixture of sunflower oil and butter. Makes enough for 8 herring, 4 mackerel or 4 fillets of salmon.

Polenta

Mix 2 teaspoons chopped thyme (or 1 teaspoon paprika if you want it hot) with 100 g (3½ oz/⅔ cup) polenta, salt and freshly ground black pepper and the finely grated zest of 1 lemon. Mix together 1 egg and 1 tablespoon milk. Dip flattened boneless, skinless chicken breasts, fish fillets or fishcakes into the egg mixture and then in the polenta mixture. Fry in oil. Makes enough for 4 fish or chicken breasts.

Parmesan breadcrumbs & seeds

Mix 100 g (3½ oz/1 cup) dry brown breadcrumbs with 75 g (2¾ oz/¾ cup) grated parmesan, 1 tablespoon chopped parsley, 2 tablespoons linseeds (flax seeds), salt and pepper. Dip boneless, skinless chicken thighs or fish fillets into 2 beaten eggs and then in the breadcrumb mixture. Place the fillets on a baking tray and cook in an oven preheated to 180°C (350°F) for 40 minutes (chicken thighs) or 15–20 minutes (fish fillets). Makes enough for 6 pieces.

Sesame seeds

Make goujons by coating finger-length pieces of fish or chicken in white sesame seeds. Using 500 g (1 lb 2 oz) boneless, skinless chicken breasts or fish fillets, dip the pieces in 2 lightly beaten egg whites and then into 155 g (5½ oz/1 cup) white sesame seeds. Season. Fry in oil and drain on paper towel. Makes enough for 4 servings.

Couscous & saffron crust

Cover 225 g (8 oz) wholemeal (whole-wheat) couscous with 300 ml (10 fl oz) boiling water mixed with a pinch of saffron. Season well. Cover with plastic wrap, set aside until the liquid is absorbed and then fork the couscous. Beat together 1 egg with 1 tablespoon milk. Dip 4 fish fillets or boneless, skinless chicken breasts into the egg mixture and then into the couscous, coating both sides. Drizzle with olive oil. Bake for 15–20 minutes (fish fillets) or 25 minutes (chicken) at 190°C (375°F). Serves 4.

PETIT SALÉ AUX LENTILLES

This is an old-fashioned classic. You could serve this with root vegetables as well as lentils – just cook some in the stock in which the petit salé is simmered.

FROM THE GROCER

200 g (7 oz) coarse sea salt

15 g (½ oz) soft brown sugar

5 dried bay leaves

1 teaspoon cloves

1 teaspoon allspice berries

2 teaspoons juniper berries

8 black peppercorns

15 g (½ oz) butter

250 g (9 oz) puy (tiny blue-green) lentils, drained and rinsed

freshly ground black pepper

FROM THE GREENGROCER

1½ onions

4 carrots

5 celery stalks

a handful of parsley stalks

1 garlic clove, finely chopped

1 thyme sprig

1 tablespoon finely chopped flat-leaf (Italian) parsley, plus extra for sprinkling

FROM THE BUTCHER

1 kg (2 lb 3 oz) piece of fatty pork belly, rind on

Place the sea salt, sugar, 2 of the bay leaves, the cloves, allspice berries and juniper berries in a food processor and blitz. Alternatively, pound in a mortar. Place the pork in a plastic container and rub half the salt mixture all over, massaging well. Cover and leave to cure for 4 hours, then rinse well.

Roughly chop the 1 whole onion, 2 of the carrots and 4 of the celery stalks. Place in a saucepan with the pork, 2 of the bay leaves, the parsley stalks and the peppercorns, and cover with cold water. Slowly bring to the boil, skim the surface, then reduce the heat and simmer very gently for 1 hour 30 minutes, or until the pork is completely tender. Strain off about 600 ml (20½ fl oz) of the cooking water – enough to cover the lentils – and discard the cooked vegetables. Leave the pork in the pan with the remaining water.

Finely chop the ½ onion and dice the remaining celery and carrots. Melt the butter in a saucepan over a medium–low heat and sauté the diced onion, celery and carrots until soft but not coloured. Add the garlic and cook gently for 1 minute, then add the remaining bay leaf, the thyme sprig, lentils and the reserved pork cooking water. Bring to the boil, reduce the heat and cook until the lentils are tender but still have a little bite, about 15–20 minutes. All the stock should have been absorbed when they are done. Remove the bay leaf and thyme and stir in the chopped parsley. Check the lentils for seasoning.

Gently reheat the pork in its cooking water, then lift it out of the pan, shaking off any excess liquid, and onto a board. Carve it into thick slices. Serve each person a pile of lentils and top with a slice of pork and a sprinkling of parsley.

PIG'S CHEEKS
WITH BARLEY & WHOLEGRAIN MUSTARD LENTILS

Pig's cheeks need to be cooked long and slow but they are worth the effort as the resulting meat is unbelievably tender. They aren't easy to find but get your butcher to source them for you.

FROM THE GROCER

seasoned plain (all-purpose) flour, for dusting

1 tablespoon peanut oil

100 ml (3½ fl oz) dry white wine

275 ml (9½ fl oz) chicken or beef stock

200 g (7 oz) pearl barley

100 ml (3½ fl oz) olive oil

salt and freshly ground black pepper

30 g (1 oz) butter

225 g (8 oz) puy (tiny blue-green) lentils, drained and rinsed

1 dried bay leaf

100 ml (3½ fl oz) thick (double/heavy) cream

2½ tablespoons wholegrain mustard

FROM THE GREENGROCER

70 ml (2¼ fl oz) lemon juice

2 onions, finely chopped

2 celery stalks, finely chopped

2 garlic cloves, finely chopped

2 tablespoons chopped flat-leaf (Italian) parsley, plus extra leaves to garnish

grated zest of ½ lemon

FROM THE BUTCHER

12 pig's cheeks, trimmed

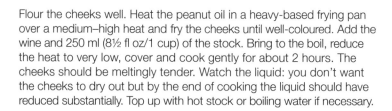

Flour the cheeks well. Heat the peanut oil in a heavy-based frying pan over a medium–high heat and fry the cheeks until well-coloured. Add the wine and 250 ml (8½ fl oz/1 cup) of the stock. Bring to the boil, reduce the heat to very low, cover and cook gently for about 2 hours. The cheeks should be meltingly tender. Watch the liquid: you don't want the cheeks to dry out but by the end of cooking the liquid should have reduced substantially. Top up with hot stock or boiling water if necessary.

Put the barley in a saucepan and cover with water. Bring to the boil, reduce the heat and simmer until tender, about 30–40 minutes. Drain. Stir in 80 ml (2½ fl oz/⅓ cup) of the olive oil, salt and pepper and 2 tablespoons of the lemon juice while the barley is still warm. Set aside.

Put the remaining olive oil and half the butter into a large saucepan over a medium heat and sauté half of the onions and half of the celery stalks until soft. Add the garlic and cook for another 2 minutes. Add the barley and the remaining stock, stir and heat to boiling. Stir in the parsley and the lemon zest, and taste for seasoning.

To cook the lentils, melt the remaining butter in a saucepan over a medium–low heat and gently sauté the remaining onion and celery until soft but not coloured. Add the lentils, bay leaf and 450 ml (15 fl oz) water and bring to the boil. Turn the heat down and simmer for 20 minutes, or until tender. Drain and remove the bay leaf.

Put the cream in a large saucepan and bring to the boil. Reduce the heat to a simmer and add the mustard, the remaining lemon juice and seasoning. Add the lentils and stir everything together.

If necessary, lift out the cheeks and reduce the juices. Serve with some of the cooking juices and the mustard lentils and barley alongside. Garnish with parsley leaves.

SPICED PORK BELLY
WITH PUY LENTILS, KAMUT & PRESERVED LEMON

This is a very gutsy ensemble, with flavours from both India and the Middle East. Kamut, though lovely and nutty, needs really good seasoning and strong flavours to go with it, hence the use of preserved lemons.

FROM THE GROCER

1½ tablespoons cumin seeds

1½ teaspoons dried chilli flakes

3 teaspoons dried thyme

3 teaspoons sea salt flakes

100 ml (3½ fl oz) olive oil

600 ml (20½ fl oz) dry white wine

250 g (9 oz) kamut, soaked overnight in cold water and drained

2 teaspoons ground cumin

300 g (10½ oz) puy (tiny blue-green) or other green lentils, drained and rinsed

450 ml (15 fl oz) chicken stock or water

salt and freshly ground black pepper

2 teaspoons red wine vinegar

80 ml (2½ fl oz/⅓ cup) extra-virgin olive oil

rind from 2 preserved lemons, finely shredded, plus 2 tablespoons juice from the jar

FROM THE GREENGROCER

1 small onion, very finely chopped

4 garlic cloves, finely chopped

1 carrot, finely chopped

2 large tomatoes, chopped

5 tablespoons chopped coriander (cilantro)

FROM THE BUTCHER

1.5 kg (3 lb 5 oz) pork belly, rind scored

Crush the cumin seeds, 1 teaspoon of the chilli flakes, the thyme and sea salt flakes using a mortar and pestle. Stir in 60 ml (2 fl oz/¼ cup) of the olive oil. Rub the mixture all over the pork, cover with foil and refrigerate for 1 hour. Remove 45 minutes before cooking.

Preheat the oven to 220°C (430°F). Roast the pork, skin side up, for 30 minutes. Reduce the heat to 170°C (340°F) and pour half the wine round the pork. Cook for a further 1 hour 30 minutes, pouring the rest of the wine round the meat 30 minutes before the end.

Meanwhile put the kamut into a saucepan and cover with water. Bring to the boil, reduce the heat to a brisk simmer and cook for 50–60 minutes, or until tender. Make sure the grain is covered with liquid throughout. When done, the grains should be plump and soft but still firm in the centre. Drain.

Heat the remaining olive oil in a heavy-based saucepan over a low heat and gently sauté the onion for 10 minutes. Add the garlic, ground cumin and remaining chilli flakes, and sauté for 2 minutes. Add the carrot, tomatoes, lentils and stock and bring to the boil. Immediately reduce the heat to a simmer, season and cook, covered, for 25 minutes, or until the lentils are tender and the liquid has been completely absorbed. You may need to add a little more liquid to stop them drying out. Carefully stir in the vinegar, 2 tablespoons of the extra-virgin olive oil and 2 tablespoons of the coriander and cover to keep warm.

Using a fork, mix the remaining extra-virgin olive oil, the preserved lemon rind, the juice from the jar and the remaining coriander into the kamut. Season well.

When done, transfer the pork to a warm plate and cover tightly with foil. Tip the lentils onto a serving platter, carve the pork into thick slices and place on top. Serve with the kamut and the juices from the roasting tin.

OREGANO & LEMON PORK CHOPS
WITH GARLICKY SPLIT PEA PURÉE & TABOULEH

The split pea purée here is also very good made into a soup – just add stock – or serve it at room temperature as part of a mezze spread.

FROM THE GROCER

150 ml (5 fl oz) olive oil

3 teaspoons dried oregano

salt and freshly ground black pepper

250 g (9 oz) split peas

2 dried bay leaves

2 small dried red chillies, crumbled

2 teaspoons ground allspice

75–90 ml (2½–3 fl oz) extra-virgin olive oil, plus extra for drizzling

150 g (5½ oz) burghul (bulgur wheat)

FROM THE GREENGROCER

juice of 3–4 lemons

2 white onions

8 garlic cloves, finely chopped

¼ small red onion, shaved

2 ripe roma (plum) tomatoes, peeled, seeded and diced

½ cucumber, seeded and diced

25 g (1 oz) finely chopped flat-leaf (Italian) parsley

15 g (½ oz) finely chopped mint

2 shallots, finely chopped

lemon wedges, to serve

FROM THE BUTCHER

6 quality pork chops, about 300 g (10½ oz) each, bone in, some fat on

Arrange the chops in a single layer in a dish. Pour over 90 ml (3 fl oz) of the olive oil and the juice of 1 of the lemons. Sprinkle with the oregano, salt and pepper. Rub this marinade all over the chops. Cover with plastic wrap and refrigerate for a few hours, or a minimum of 30 minutes.

Cut 1 of the white onions in half and place in a saucepan with the split peas and bay leaves. Cover with 1.5 litres (51 fl oz/6 cups) water. Bring to the boil, skim the surface, reduce the heat to very low and simmer uncovered for about 30 minutes. The peas should collapse into a thick purée. If the mixture is too thin, simmer uncovered until it reaches the consistency you want. Set aside.

Finely chop the remaining white onion and cook in the remaining olive oil in a saucepan over a medium–low heat until soft but not coloured. Add three-quarters of the garlic and cook for 6 minutes, or until the garlic is completely soft. Add the chillies and allspice and cook for another couple of minutes, then scrape this into the pea purée. Season well and stir in the juice of 1 of the lemons and 2 tablespoons of the extra-virgin olive oil. Scatter the shaved red onion on top and drizzle with a little more extra-virgin olive oil.

Preheat the oven to 190°C (375°F). Let the chops come to room temperature if you've had them in the refrigerator. Roast for 20 minutes.

To make the tabouleh, soak the burghul in enough cold water to cover by 3 cm (1¼ in) for 15 minutes. Drain, tip into a clean tea towel (dish towel) and squeeze out the moisture. Spread the burghul on a baking tray to dry for 20 minutes. Transfer to a large bowl and mix in the tomatoes, cucumber, parsley, mint, shallots and the remaining garlic cloves. Gradually add the remaining extra-virgin olive oil and lemon juice. You want the burghul to be coated, not drowned, in dressing. Season to taste.

Warm the purée and serve with the chops and tabouleh. Offer wedges of lemon on the side.

SAFFRON-GLAZED CHICKEN
WITH JEWELLED COUSCOUS

This is actually a very simple dish but the 'jewels' make it very sumptuous.

FROM THE GROCER

½ teaspoon saffron threads
dissolved in 2 tablespoons
boiling water

125 g (4½ oz) butter, melted

salt and freshly ground black pepper

75 g (2¾ oz) mixed dried figs
and apricots

50 g (1¾ oz) dried sour cherries

25 g (1 oz) dried cranberries
or barberries

225 g (8 oz) wholemeal (whole-
wheat) couscous

225 ml (7½ fl oz) chicken stock

1 tablespoon olive oil

1 teaspoon mixed (pumpkin pie)
spice

100 g (3½ oz) unsalted pistachio
nuts, roughly chopped

1–2 tablespoons extra-virgin olive oil

FROM THE GREENGROCER

a good squeeze of lemon

½ onion, chopped

1 garlic clove, finely chopped

30 g (1 oz) fresh coriander (cilantro),
mint or flat-leaf (Italian)
parsley, roughly
chopped

seeds from 1 pomegranate

FROM THE BUTCHER

1 x 2 kg (4 lb 6 oz) roasting
chicken

Preheat the oven to 180°C (350°F). In a small pitcher, combine the saffron and its water, the butter and lemon juice. Season the chicken inside and out, place in a roasting tin and pour over half of the buttery saffron mixture. Roast for 1 hour 40 minutes, basting occasionally with the remaining saffron butter and tin juices. Reserve a little of the saffron mixture to pour over the chicken just before serving.

About 30 minutes before the chicken is cooked, cover the dried fruit with water in a saucepan. Bring to the boil, remove from the heat and set aside for 15 minutes. Drain and roughly chop any large bits of fruit.

Put the couscous into a large bowl. Heat the chicken stock to boiling and pour over the couscous. Cover with plastic wrap and leave to plump up for about 15 minutes.

Meanwhile, sauté the onion in the olive oil in a saucepan over a medium heat until translucent. Add the garlic, mixed spice and the soaked dried fruit and cook for 1 minute. Add this to the couscous, along with the pistachio nuts, herbs and extra-virgin olive oil. Gently fork through and check for seasoning.

Transfer the couscous to a large platter or shallow bowl and scatter over the pomegranate seeds just before serving. Place the chicken on top and drizzle over the remaining saffron mixture. Pour the buttery juices from the roasting tin into a warm pitcher and serve alongside.

OLD-FASHIONED ROAST GUINEA FOWL
WITH LENTILS & BACON

You may have a chunk of protein here but the lentils really make this dish – it's such a classic pairing. Braised lettuce is lovely on the side.

FROM THE GROCER

40 g (1½ oz) butter, slightly softened

2 tablespoons olive oil

400 g (14 oz) puy (tiny blue-green) lentils, drained and rinsed

2 dried bay leaves

600 ml (20½ fl oz) light chicken or vegetable stock, or water

salt and freshly ground black pepper

1 teaspoon sherry vinegar

1 tablespoon extra-virgin olive oil

FROM THE GREENGROCER

½ onion, very finely chopped

1 celery stalk, diced

1 large carrot, diced

2 garlic cloves, finely chopped

3 thyme sprigs

1½ tablespoons chopped flat-leaf (Italian) parsley

watercress, to serve (optional)

FROM THE BUTCHER

2 guinea fowls

200 g (7 oz) smoked lardons

Preheat the oven to 190°C (375°F). Season the insides of the guinea fowls and rub them all over with some of the butter. Gently lift the skin on the breasts, push some more butter underneath and season the outside. Roast the birds for 1 hour; they are cooked when the juices between the thigh and breast run clear.

Heat the olive oil in a saucepan over a medium–low heat and gently sauté the lardons until golden. Reduce the heat, add the onion, celery, carrot and garlic, and cook until the onion is soft but not coloured. Add the lentils, mixing them through the pan juices. Drop in the thyme sprigs and the bay leaves, pour on the stock and season lightly with salt and pepper. Bring to the boil, then reduce the heat and simmer uncovered until the lentils are just tender and the stock has been absorbed, about 20–30 minutes. Fish out the thyme sprigs and the bay leaves. Check the seasoning and gently stir through the vinegar and extra-virgin olive oil.

Gently reheat the lentils and add the parsley. Tip the lentils onto a warm platter and place the guinea fowls on top, or serve the lentils in a warm bowl and the guinea fowls on a separate platter with clumps of very fresh watercress (if using). Serve with the cooking juices from the birds.

PROVENÇAL CHICKEN
WITH CAMARGUE RED RICE STUFFING

The sweet–savoury flavours of the stuffing might make you think this is a Spanish or a Middle Eastern dish but it is actually from Provence. You don't need to serve it with any more starch, but spinach or roast cherry tomatoes are good on the side.

FROM THE GROCER

30 g (1 oz) butter

80 ml (2½ fl oz/⅓ cup) olive oil

50 g (1¾ oz/⅓ cup) pine nuts, toasted

50 g (1¾ oz) raisins

250 g (9 oz) Camargue red rice

600 ml (20½ fl oz) chicken stock

salt and freshly ground black pepper

1 teaspoon cayenne pepper

sea salt flakes

FROM THE GREENGROCER

2 onions, roughly chopped

2 garlic cloves, crushed

grated zest of 1 lemon

2 thyme sprigs, leaves picked

FROM THE BUTCHER

1 x 2 kg (4 lb 6 oz) roasting chicken

Heat the butter and 1 tablespoon of the olive oil in a saucepan and cook the onions over a medium heat until soft and pale gold. Add the garlic and cook for 2 minutes more, then stir in the pine nuts, raisins, lemon zest, thyme leaves and rice. Mix the rice through the buttery juices to coat well and add the stock. Bring to the boil, reduce the heat and season with salt and pepper. Simmer for about 45 minutes. Keep checking the rice during cooking – it should absorb all the stock and end up moist but not dry. Add some boiling water if necessary. Check the seasoning – rice always needs lots – and leave to cool.

Preheat the oven to 180°C (350°F). Season the chicken inside, then spoon the rice stuffing right down into the cavity. Set the chicken in a roasting tin and pour over the remaining olive oil, rubbing it all over the skin. Sprinkle with the cayenne pepper, black pepper and sea salt flakes. Roast for 1 hour 40 minutes. The chicken should be golden and the stuffing should have softened even more.

DIP Turkish or Middle Eastern bread into olive oil and then into this colourful and fragrant spice mix. Or do as they do in Egypt, and dip hard-boiled hen or quail eggs into the dukka.

how to
MAKE DUKKA

1 Put 200 g (7 oz) blanched hazelnuts into a dry frying pan and toast until golden. Be careful not to go too far – they burn very easily. Tip them onto a plate immediately to let them cool down.

2 Put 100 g (3½ oz/⅔ cup) white sesame seeds into the frying pan and toast them in the same way. As they are smaller they will cook even more quickly. Transfer to a plate.

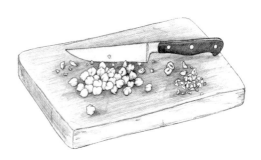

3 Toast 40 g (1½ oz) coriander seeds, 3 tablespoons cumin seeds and 2 tablespoons sunflower kernels in the frying pan until you can smell the fragrance of the spices.

4 Roughly chop the hazelnuts with a sharp knife – you want to end up with a coarse, chunky mixture.

5 Coarsely grind the sesame seeds, sunflower kernels, coriander and cumin seeds in a mortar with ½ teaspoon black peppercorns and 1 teaspoon flaked sea salt. Don't overdo the grinding – you want a crunchy texture.

6 Combine the seeds with the hazelnuts and 2 teaspoons ground paprika. Keep in an airtight container – the mixture will be good for 6–8 weeks.

SEARED LAMB FILLET
WITH LIGURIAN BROAD BEAN PESTO

The star here – the bread with the broad bean pesto – can also be served with fish such as red mullet or bream fillets. Despite the name, Ligurian bean pesto is usually served with bread or protein rather than pasta.

FROM THE GROCER

5 tinned anchovies

4 tablespoons grated pecorino

180 ml (6 fl oz) extra-virgin olive oil, plus extra for drizzling (optional)

salt and freshly ground black pepper

60 ml (2 fl oz/¼ cup) olive oil

mustard, to serve (optional)

FROM THE GREENGROCER

500 g (1 lb 2 oz) young broad (fava) beans (podded weight)

2 garlic cloves, crushed

12 mint leaves, chopped

juice of ½ lemon, or to taste

400 g (14 oz) cherry tomatoes on the vine

FROM THE BUTCHER

2 x 300 g (10½ oz) lamb fillets, trimmed

FROM THE BAKER

8 slices ciabatta

For the pesto, boil the podded broad beans in water until tender, about 4 minutes. Drain, rinse in cold water and slip the beans from their skins. Place in a food processor and add the garlic, mint, anchovies and pecorino. Pulse while very slowly adding the extra-virgin olive oil. Taste and season with salt and pepper. Add the lemon juice and taste for seasoning again. Set aside.

Preheat the oven to 200°C (400°F). Put the cherry tomatoes into a baking dish, drizzle over 1 tablespoon of the olive oil and turn the tomatoes to coat. Season with salt and pepper and roast for 15 minutes, or until the tomatoes are soft and slightly charred. Snip the branch so that you have 4 sprigs, one for each serving.

Sprinkle the lamb with pepper, heat the remaining olive oil in a frying pan and brown the meat all over. Transfer to a roasting tin, season with salt and roast for 10 minutes. Remove from the oven, cover and keep warm for 10 minutes while the meat rests.

Toast the ciabatta on both sides – preferably on a chargrill pan so you end up with lovely stripes – and drizzle with extra-virgin olive oil. Spread the pesto thickly on top. Cut the lamb into thick slices and serve on warm plates alongside the ciabatta. Top the ciabatta with a sprig of tomatoes, drizzle over more extra-virgin olive oil and serve with some mustard alongside, if desired.

WARM CHICKPEA & ONION PURÉE
WITH SIZZLING CAPSICUM, LAMB & MINT

There's a bit of juggling here to get all the elements on the table together but the recipe itself isn't taxing. Serve with flatbread, Greek-style yoghurt and other mezze dishes.

FROM THE GROCER

275 ml (9½ fl oz) olive oil

1½ tablespoons cumin seeds

3 teaspoons ground cinnamon

800 g (1 lb 12 oz) tinned chickpeas (garbanzo beans), drained and rinsed

salt and freshly ground black pepper

90 g (3 oz/⅓ cup) tahini

1½ tablespoons cayenne pepper

80 ml (2½ fl oz/⅓ cup) extra-virgin olive oil

FROM THE GREENGROCER

1 large onion, finely chopped

8 garlic cloves, chopped

juice of 2 lemons, plus a squeeze of lemon

3 red capsicums (bell peppers), halved, seeded and sliced into 1 cm (½ in) strips

a handful of fresh mint leaves, torn

FROM THE BUTCHER

2 x 300 g (10½ oz) lamb fillets

To make the purée, heat 2 tablespoons of the olive oil in a large frying pan over a medium–low heat and sauté the onion until soft but not coloured. Add the garlic, cumin seeds and cinnamon and cook for another 2 minutes. Add the chickpeas and salt and pepper and cook for a couple of minutes more so the flavours combine. Tip into a food processor or blender and add all but 2 tablespoons of the remaining olive oil, the lemon juice, 150 ml (5 fl oz) water, salt and pepper and the tahini. Blend to a smooth purée, adding more water if necessary. You may want to add more tahini, lemon juice or oil. Set aside.

Cut the lamb into strips and season with salt, pepper and cayenne pepper.

Heat 1 tablespoon of the olive oil in a large frying pan and fry the capsicum strips over a high heat until slightly scorched in patches. Reduce the heat and continue cooking until they are cooked right through and soft. Season.

When the capsicum is nearly ready, start to gently warm the chickpea purée. At the same time, heat the remaining olive oil in a separate frying pan and fry the lamb over a high heat until it has a good colour – this should take a matter of minutes.

Transfer the warm purée into a broad shallow bowl and scatter the capsicum and lamb over the top. Quickly but gently heat the extra-virgin olive oil and drop in the mint leaves. Let the mint infuse for a few moments on the heat, and then pour the oil over the chickpea purée, lamb and capsicum. Add a squeeze of lemon and serve immediately.

CHARGRILLED LAMB CHOPS
WITH BUTTERBEAN & BROWN RICE PILAFF

This dish uses the flavours of Catalonia, where fruity *alioli* based on pears, apples or quinces is very common. You can use kale or savoy cabbage instead of cavolo nero if you prefer.

FROM THE GROCER

½ teaspoon rock salt

70 ml (2¼ fl oz) mild extra-virgin olive oil

1 teaspoon white wine vinegar

1½ tablespoons runny honey

250 g (9 oz) mixture of brown basmati and wild rice

25 g (1 oz) butter

about 700 ml (23½ fl oz) chicken stock

1 tablespoon olive oil, plus extra for brushing

400 g (14 oz) tinned butterbeans, drained and rinsed

salt and freshly ground black pepper

FROM THE GREENGROCER

2 granny smith apples, peeled, cored and cut into chunks

4 garlic cloves

1 onion, finely chopped

150 g (5½ oz) cavolo nero, shredded

FROM THE BUTCHER

6 large lamb chump chops

To make the *alioli*, put the apples in a small saucepan, cover with water and cook until very tender. Drain. Cut 2 of the garlic cloves in half and crush with the rock salt in a large mortar. Add the cooked apples and crush until smooth. Add the extra-virgin olive oil a drop at a time, beating constantly until you have a thick purée. Add the vinegar and the honey. Refrigerate until needed.

Rinse the rice in a sieve until the water runs clear. Heat 15 g (½ oz) of the butter in a heavy-based saucepan over a medium heat and sauté the onion until soft and pale gold. Add the remaining garlic (finely chopped) and cook for another couple of minutes. Stir in the rice and cook until it just begins to toast. Add 500 ml (17 fl oz/2 cups) of the stock, bring to the boil and cook until the rice starts to look pitted. Reduce the heat to very low and cover – the rice will now steam. Top up with stock every so often and gently fork occasionally to make sure the rice doesn't stick to the bottom of the pan. It should cook in about 30 minutes. Brown rice never softens as much as white rice – it will still be a little firm in the centre – and wild rice stays even firmer.

Meanwhile, blanch the cavolo nero in boiling water for 4 minutes. Drain. Heat the remaining butter and the 1 tablespoon olive oil in a large frying pan over a medium heat, add the beans and the cavolo nero and warm through. Season. When the rice is cooked, remove from the heat and fork through the cavolo nero and beans. Check the seasoning and cover to keep warm.

Just before serving, heat a chargrill pan until very hot. Brush the chops with olive oil and season. Sear each side over a high heat, then turn the heat down to cook them through. I prefer them rare – about 4 minutes each side – but cook to the degree of doneness you like. Just insert a small sharp knife into the flesh of a chop to check the meat.

Spoon a portion of pilaff onto each plate, top with a lamb chop and a good dollop of *alioli*. Serve the rest of the pilaff and *alioli* on the side.

LEEK, SPINACH & GRUYÈRE TART
WITH SPELT PASTRY

This is quite a light tart, even though the pastry is made from spelt flour. If you want to make a non-vegetarian version you can add sautéed lardons.

FROM THE GROCER

165 g (6 oz) butter

130 g (4½ oz) white spelt flour, plus extra for dusting

125 g (4½ oz) brown spelt flour

salt and freshly ground black pepper

3 large eggs, lightly beaten, plus 1 egg yolk

2½ tablespoons milk

250 ml (8½ fl oz/1 cup) thick (double/heavy) cream

freshly grated nutmeg

100 g (3½ oz/¾ cup) grated gruyère

FROM THE GREENGROCER

300 g (10½ oz) English spinach, washed and large stalks removed

2 leeks, white part only, thinly sliced

For the pastry, cut 150 g (5½ oz) of the butter into cubes and place in a food processor with the flours and a pinch of salt. Process until the mixture looks like breadcrumbs. Add the egg yolk and process again until the mixture forms a ball. Wrap in plastic wrap and refrigerate for 2 hours.

Preheat the oven to 200°C (400°F) and place a baking tray inside. Dust a work surface with flour and roll out the dough to fit a 24 cm (9½ in) flan (tart) tin that is 4 cm (1½ in) deep. Line the tin with the dough and place in the freezer or the coldest part of the refrigerator for 20 minutes. When chilled, prick the base with a fork, line with baking paper and fill with baking beans. Place in the oven on the baking tray and bake for 7 minutes. Remove the paper and beans and bake for a further 7 minutes. Remove from the oven. Reduce the oven to 180°C (350°F) and leave the baking tray inside.

For the filling, put the spinach into a pan with just the water clinging to it after washing. Cover, set over a low heat and cook for about 4 minutes, tossing it a couple of times. Drain and leave to cool completely.

Melt the remaining butter in a heavy-based saucepan over a medium heat, add the leeks and stir well. Add 2 tablespoons water, cover, reduce the heat and sweat for 15 minutes. When the leeks are completely soft, remove the lid and boil off the excess liquid. Squeeze the water out of the spinach – press between two dinner plates to remove as much liquid as possible. Chop the spinach, add to the leeks and taste for seasoning.

Mix together the milk, cream and the beaten eggs. Season and add the nutmeg. Spread the spinach and leeks in the tart case and scatter over the gruyère. Slowly pour in the milk and cream mixture. Slide the tart into the oven onto the hot baking tray and bake for 30–40 minutes, or until just set in the middle. Leave to rest for about 15 minutes – it will continue to cook a little in the residual heat.

ROQUEFORT, ONION & WALNUT TART

Using half wholemeal (whole-wheat) and half plain (all-purpose) flour makes a lighter pastry than using all wholemeal flour. Serve this with a pear and watercress salad. It will go beautifully with the Roquefort in the tart.

FROM THE GROCER

150 g (5½ oz) butter

125 g (4½ oz) wholemeal (whole-wheat) flour

125 g (4½ oz) plain (all-purpose) flour, plus extra for dusting

¼ teaspoon salt

2 large eggs, plus 3 egg yolks

2 teaspoons caster (superfine) sugar (optional)

225 ml (7½ fl oz) thick (double/heavy) cream

75 ml (2½ fl oz) milk

freshly ground black pepper

a good grating of nutmeg

100 g (3½ oz) Roquefort or other blue cheese, crumbled

2 tablespoons olive oil

125 g (4½ oz/1¼ cups) walnut halves

2 tablespoons walnut oil

FROM THE GREENGROCER

4 large onions, very finely sliced

4 garlic cloves, sliced

3 tablespoons roughly chopped flat-leaf (Italian) parsley

Preheat the oven to 200°C (400°F). Put 125 g (4½ oz) of the butter, both flours and the salt into a food processor fitted with a plastic blade. Process until the mixture resembles breadcrumbs. Add 1 of the egg yolks mixed with 1 tablespoon very cold water and process again until the dough forms a ball. Wrap in plastic wrap and refrigerate for a couple of hours.

Return the dough to room temperature and roll out on a lightly floured surface until large enough to fit a 25 cm (10 in) flan (tart) tin that is 3 cm (1¼ in) deep. Place the dough in the flan tin and chill for 20 minutes. Line the pastry case with baking paper, fill with baking beans and bake for 10 minutes. Remove the baking paper and beans and bake for another 5 minutes. Set aside to cool.

Heat the remaining butter in a heavy-based saucepan over a low heat and cook the onions, stirring, for about 5 minutes. Add a splash of water, cover and cook until the onions are really soft and dark gold, about 30–40 minutes. Keep checking on them to make sure they are not catching on the bottom of the pan. Turn the heat up and continue to cook, stirring, until caramelised. If it's difficult to get them to this stage, sprinkle over a couple of teaspoons of sugar to help the process along. Set aside.

Mix the 2 whole eggs and the remaining 2 egg yolks, the cream and milk together and season with pepper and nutmeg.

Spread the onions in the bottom of the pastry case and scatter over the Roquefort. Pour the egg mixture over the top. Reduce the oven to 190°C (375°F) and bake for 40–45 minutes, or until the tart is golden and the centre just set. Remove from the oven and leave to cool for about 10 minutes.

Heat the olive oil in a frying pan and add the garlic and walnuts. Stir-fry until the garlic is golden and the walnuts lightly toasted. Stir in the walnut oil and the parsley. Serve the tart warm with the walnut and garlic mixture spooned over the top.

ROAST VEGETABLES
WITH WHITE BEAN SKORDALIA

Skordalia is a thick garlic dip or dressing popular in Greece and Turkey. Some versions are based on potatoes and many are made with nuts, but this bean version is particularly healthy.

FROM THE GROCER

180 ml (6 fl oz) olive oil, plus extra for drizzling

800 g (1 lb 12 oz) tinned cannellini (lima) beans, drained and rinsed

salt and freshly ground black pepper

150 ml (5 fl oz) extra-virgin olive oil, plus extra for drizzling

FROM THE GREENGROCER

½ white onion, roughly chopped

4 garlic cloves, crushed

a good squeeze of lemon

3 red capsicums (bell peppers), halved and seeded

2 yellow capsicums (bell peppers), halved and seeded

1 large eggplant (aubergine)

3 zucchini (courgettes)

12 roma (plum) tomatoes

2 small red onions

8 thyme sprigs (optional)

For the skordalia, heat 2 tablespoons of the olive oil in a saucepan over a medium–low heat and gently cook the white onion until soft but not coloured. Add the garlic and cook for another 2 minutes until the garlic is soft. Transfer to a blender or food processor. Add the beans and salt and pepper, then purée while adding the extra-virgin olive oil. Add the squeeze of lemon and adjust the seasoning; you might want to add more lemon as well as salt and pepper. Cover and set aside until ready to serve.

Preheat the oven to 190ºC (375ºF). Cut the capsicum halves lengthways into 4 broad strips. Cut the eggplant into rounds; quarter the largest slices and halve the rest. Thickly slice the zucchini and halve the tomatoes. Halve the red onions and cut each half into 1.5 cm (½ in) slices. Put the vegetables into a roasting tin large enough to accommodate them in a single layer. Pour over the remaining olive oil and turn the vegetables to coat. Add the thyme sprigs (if using) and season. Roast for 40 minutes, or until soft and slightly charred. Shake the tin and turn the vegetables a couple of times during roasting.

Serve the vegetables warm or at room temperature on a big platter alongside a bowl of the skordalia – over which you have drizzled a generous slug of extra-virgin olive oil.

EGGPLANT & LENTIL MOUSSAKA

In traditional Greek moussaka the sauce is a plain béchamel but I like to add some grated gruyère, which gives it a slight cheesy flavour. You can include this or not, the choice is yours.

FROM THE GROCER

800 g (1 lb 12 oz) tinned chopped tomatoes in thick juice

2 teaspoons sugar

about 90 ml (3 fl oz) olive oil

245 g (8½ oz/1⅓ cups) green lentils, drained and rinsed

salt and freshly ground black pepper

800 ml (27 fl oz) milk

1 dried bay leaf

8 black peppercorns

freshly grated nutmeg, to taste

85 g (3 oz) butter

75 g (2¾ oz/½ cup) plain (all-purpose) flour

75 g (2¾ oz) gruyère, grated (optional)

75 g (2¾ oz/¾ cup) grated parmesan or pecorino

FROM THE GREENGROCER

1 onion, finely chopped, plus ½ onion

2 garlic cloves, crushed

1 celery stalk, very finely chopped

3 oregano sprigs, leaves picked

4 large eggplants (aubergines)

a few parsley stalks

Place the chopped onion, garlic, celery, tomatoes, sugar, oregano leaves and 2 tablespoons of the olive oil in a saucepan. Bring to the boil, reduce the heat to medium–low and cook for 10 minutes. Add 250 ml (8½ fl oz/1 cup) water and the lentils, and stir well. Cook for 25–30 minutes, or until the lentils are soft and the sauce is quite thick. Check for seasoning.

Meanwhile, cut the green tops off the eggplants and cut them lengthways into slices about 5 mm (¼ in) thick. Pour some of the remaining oil into a frying pan over a medium heat and cook the eggplant in batches, adding oil sparingly as needed. Adjust the heat if necessary so that the slices are soft and golden on both sides. Transfer to paper towel as you go.

To make the béchamel sauce, heat the milk with the ½ onion, bay leaf, parsley stalks and peppercorns to boiling point. Remove from the heat and infuse for 30 minutes, strain and add some nutmeg. Melt the butter in a saucepan and add the flour, stirring to make a roux. Remove from the heat and add the warm milk a little at a time, starting off with small amounts and stirring well to incorporate. When all the milk has been added return the pan to the heat and cook, stirring all the time, until the mixture thickens and comes to the boil. Reduce the heat and simmer for 5 minutes. Add the gruyère (if using) and stir to help it melt. Season well.

Preheat the oven to 180°C (350°F). To assemble the moussaka, spread a layer of lentils in the base of an ovenproof dish and add a layer of eggplant, followed by a layer of béchamel sauce. Repeat until you have used everything up, ending with a layer of sauce. Sprinkle with the parmesan or pecorino and bake for 40 minutes, or until golden and bubbling.

sides

ZUCCHINI & FETA FRITTERS
WITH SUNFLOWER KERNELS & TOMATO SAUCE

These are addictive. Serve them as a starter, part of a mezze spread, or as a side dish with lamb.

FROM THE GROCER

400 g (14 oz) tinned cherry tomatoes in thick juice

1 teaspoon tomato passata (puréed tomatoes)

75 ml (2½ fl oz) olive oil, plus extra if needed for frying

1½ teaspoons soft light brown sugar

salt and freshly ground black pepper

35 g (1¼ oz) sunflower kernels

4 large eggs

100 g (3½ oz/⅔ cup) wholemeal (whole-wheat) flour

200 g (7 oz) feta cheese, crumbled

¼ teaspoon cayenne pepper

FROM THE GREENGROCER

5 garlic cloves

2 onions, finely chopped

3 large zucchini (courgettes), about 550 g (1 lb 3 oz), coarsely grated

10 g (¼ oz) each flat-leaf (Italian) parsley, mint and dill, chopped

To make the tomato sauce, finely chop 2 of the garlic cloves and place in a saucepan with the tomatoes, tomato passata, half of the onions, 30 ml (1 fl oz) of the olive oil, the sugar and 2½ tablespoons water. Bring to the boil, reduce the heat and simmer, uncovered, for 30 minutes, or until thick. Purée in a food processor if you want a fine sauce and refrigerate until needed.

For the fritters, place the zucchini in a colander, sprinkle with salt and leave to drain for about 30 minutes. Wrap the zucchini in a clean tea towel (dish towel) and squeeze out any excess liquid – do this really thoroughly or the fritter batter will be too wet.

Heat 30 ml (1 fl oz) of the oil in a frying pan over a medium heat and fry the remaining onion until soft. Add the zucchini and cook until the mixture starts to turn golden. Crush the remaining garlic and add to the pan with the sunflower kernels. Cook for another 3 minutes or so.

Mix together the eggs and flour, beating out any lumps. Add the zucchini mixture, feta, herbs, cayenne pepper, and salt and pepper. Mix well.

Heat the remaining oil in a frying pan over a medium heat and add about 1 heaped tablespoon of the batter, letting it spread out to form a little patty. Add more spoonfuls of batter to cook as many patties as your pan can take at one time. When each patty is set and golden underneath, flip and cook the other side, adding more oil if needed. As the patties cook, remove them to paper towel.

Serve the fritters with the tomato sauce. I prefer the sauce to be warm or at room temperature, but serve it hot if you like.

ROAST PUMPKIN
WITH RICE, PANCETTA & MUSHROOM STUFFING

These pumpkins are excellent with pork and chicken. You can also serve them as a main course with another vegetable, perhaps something green, on the side. To make a vegetarian version, just leave out the pancetta and increase the quantity of mushrooms.

FROM THE GROCER

50 g (1¾ oz) butter

200 g (7 oz) mixed brown basmati, wild rice and Camargue red rice

salt and freshly ground black pepper

500 ml (17 fl oz/2 cups) chicken stock or water

15 g (½ oz) grated parmesan

FROM THE GREENGROCER

1 onion, finely chopped

200 g (7 oz) mushrooms, chopped

2 small butternut pumpkins (squash), peeled and halved, seeded and fibre removed

rocket (arugula), to serve (optional)

FROM THE BUTCHER

75 g (2¾ oz) pancetta, chopped

Melt 15 g (½ oz) of the butter in a saucepan over a medium heat and sauté the onion until soft and golden. Add the pancetta, the mushrooms and another 10 g (¼ oz) of the butter. Sauté until everything is coloured. Stir in the mixed rice, making sure it gets coated with all the buttery juices. Season well with salt and pepper and add the chicken stock or water. Cover, bring to the boil, then reduce the heat to very low and cook for 15 minutes.

Meanwhile, preheat the oven to 190ºC (375ºF). Score a lattice pattern on the flesh of the pumpkin halves to help the heat penetrate. Place them in a roasting tin, smear the remaining butter over the flesh and season with salt and pepper. Roast for 20 minutes.

Take the pumpkin out of the oven and spoon the rice stuffing into the cavities, mixing it in with the butter that has collected. Sprinkle with the parmesan and return the tin to the oven for a further 15 minutes. The flesh of the pumpkin should become completely tender and the top golden. Serve with the rocket.

RICE, PECAN & BEAN SALAD
WITH GINGER & MAPLE DRESSING

This is excellent with summery barbecue food, especially pork. You can make it spicy by adding a couple of halved, seeded and chopped chillies, or give it even more of an American accent by adding roasted corn kernels.

FROM THE GROCER

75 g (2¾ oz) wild rice

75 g (2¾ oz) Camargue red rice

150 g (5 oz/¾ cup) brown long-grain rice

60 ml (2 fl oz/¼ cup) cider vinegar

1 teaspoon dijon mustard

90 ml (3 fl oz) peanut oil

90 ml (3 fl oz) olive oil

1 chunk of stem ginger, finely chopped, plus 1½ teaspoons of syrup from the jar

1 tablespoon maple syrup

salt and freshly ground black pepper

25 g (1 oz/¼ cup) toasted pecans, roughly chopped

FROM THE GREENGROCER

2 garlic cloves, crushed

300 g (10½ oz) green beans, trimmed and cut in half

15 g (½ oz) roughly chopped flat-leaf (Italian) parsley

4 spring onions (scallions), chopped

Cook the rice in water. The brown rice will have to be cooked on its own but the wild and Camargue rice can be cooked together. Wild rice never really softens but stays firm and nutty and should be ready in 25 minutes. The brown rice will take around 40 minutes – it stays nutty as well, but less so than the wild rice.

While the rice is cooking, whisk together the garlic, vinegar, mustard, peanut oil, olive oil, ginger, ginger syrup, maple syrup and salt and pepper. It looks like a lot of dressing but rice salads really soak it up. Set aside.

Cook the beans in boiling salted water until al dente, then plunge them into cold water to preserve their green colour. Drain. When the rice is cooked, drain and mix with the beans, pecans, parsley and spring onions. Toss together with some of the dressing – keep some back to add later as the rice cools. Taste for seasoning. Serve warm or at room temperature.

KISIR

This is wonderful with lamb or, if you want to stay vegetarian, feta or mezze dishes such as hummus.

FROM THE GROCER

60 ml (2 fl oz/¼ cup) olive oil

2 teaspoons ground cumin

1½ tablespoons tomato passata
(puréed tomatoes)

200 g (7 oz) burghul (bulgur wheat)

60–80 ml (2–2½ fl oz/¼– ⅓ cup)
extra-virgin olive oil

1½ tablespoons pomegranate
molasses

salt and freshly ground black pepper

FROM THE GREENGROCER

1 small red onion, very
finely chopped

4 garlic cloves, finely chopped

1 green chilli and 1 red chilli, halved,
seeded and finely shredded

1 tablespoon lemon juice

5 flavoursome roma (plum) tomatoes,
peeled, seeded and diced

a generous handful of mint leaves,
torn

25 g (1 oz/¾ cup) finely chopped
flat-leaf (Italian) parsley

seeds from 1 medium pomegranate

Heat the olive oil in a medium saucepan over a medium–low heat and sauté the onion until it's soft but not coloured. Add the garlic, cumin and chillies, and cook for another couple of minutes, then mix in the tomato passata. Add 120 ml (4 fl oz) water and bring to the boil, then immediately remove the pan from the heat and stir in the burghul. Cover and leave to sit until the burghul has cooled. Fork the grains gently to aerate.

For the dressing, mix together the lemon juice, extra-virgin olive oil and pomegranate molasses. Set aside.

Add the tomatoes, mint and parsley to the burghul and carefully fork together. Add the dressing a little at a time – the burghul shouldn't be dry but shouldn't be soaked in dressing either. Taste for seasoning. Fork through the pomegranate seeds just before serving.

WARM WHITE BEANS
WITH WILTED ROCKET & ONIONS

You can extend and adapt this recipe by adding roasted cherry tomatoes or cooked but still-crisp green beans.

FROM THE GROCER

75 ml (2½ fl oz) olive oil

1.2 kg (2 lb 10 oz) tinned cannellini (lima) beans, drained and well rinsed

salt and freshly ground black pepper

extra-virgin olive oil, for pouring

FROM THE GREENGROCER

2 red onions, finely sliced

3 garlic cloves, finely chopped

100 g (3½ oz) rocket (arugula), torn

a good squeeze of lemon

1 tablespoon very finely chopped flat-leaf (Italian) parsley

Heat 60 ml (2 fl oz/¼ cup) of the olive oil in a frying pan over a medium–low heat and gently sauté the onions until quite soft but not coloured. Add the garlic and cook for a further 2 minutes. Add the beans and the remaining olive oil. Season with salt and pepper and let the beans heat through and absorb the cooking juices. Add the rocket and stir through so that it wilts a little in the heat. Squeeze over the lemon and stir in the parsley. Taste – beans need a lot of seasoning. Pour in a good slug of the extra-virgin olive oil and serve.

EDAMAME
WITH CHINESE FIVE-SPICE SALT

These are great with other South-East Asian appetisers and make a nice casual start to a meal.

FROM THE GROCER

2 teaspoons Sichuan peppercorns

2 star anise

1½ teaspoons fennel seeds

½ teaspoon ground cloves

1½ teaspoons ground cinnamon

1½ teaspoons toasted black
sesame seeds

1½ teaspoons toasted white
sesame seeds

¼ teaspoon hot chilli flakes

2 teaspoons sea salt flakes

FROM THE GREENGROCER

500 g (1 lb 2 oz) fresh or frozen
edamame in their pods

To make the spice powder, toast the peppercorns, star anise and fennel seeds for 30 seconds or so in a dry frying pan over a medium heat, stirring constantly, then grind them really finely in a blender. Add the cloves and cinnamon and mix well. This makes more spice powder than you need but it will keep for about 1 month in an airtight jar, after which the flavour starts to fade gradually.

To make the five-spice salt, mix 1–2 tablespoons of the spice powder with the black and white sesame seeds, the chilli and sea salt flakes, and set aside.

Cook the edamame in their pods in lightly salted boiling water for 5 minutes, or until just tender, then drain. Drain really well by shaking the colander. Tip into a bowl and toss with the five-spice salt. Diners should shell their own beans. Offer more of the five-spice salt on the side.

TUSCAN BEANS

These beans are deeply savoury and very moreish – a great dish for very little money and very little effort. Don't stint on seasoning or olive oil – the oil makes the beans all the richer.

FROM THE GROCER

300 g (10½ oz/1½ cups) dried cannellini (lima) beans, soaked overnight, rinsed and drained

1 dried bay leaf

80 ml (2½ fl oz/⅓ cup) olive oil

400 g (14 oz) tinned cherry tomatoes in thick juice

salt and freshly ground black pepper

a generous slug of extra-virgin olive oil, plus extra for drizzling

FROM THE GREENGROCER

1 small onion, halved, plus 1 onion, finely chopped

3 thyme sprigs

4 garlic cloves, finely chopped

a small handful of thyme, sage, oregano or basil, chopped (optional)

Place the beans in a saucepan, cover with cold water and add the onion halves, bay leaf and thyme sprigs. Bring to the boil, immediately reduce the heat and simmer for 1 hour. The beans will be soft but not falling apart. Drain, discard the herbs and onion halves and set aside.

Heat the olive oil in a saucepan over a medium–low heat and add the chopped onion. Gently cook until soft but not coloured. Add the garlic and cook for a couple of minutes without colouring. Add the tomatoes, bring to the boil, then reduce the heat and simmer for about 20 minutes. Don't stir too much during this time – the tomatoes should retain a bit of shape even though they are soft.

Add the cannellini beans and salt and pepper, stir and cook gently for 20–30 minutes until the beans become even more tender. The mixture should be really rich and oily although the beans shouldn't become a purée. Add the slug of extra-virgin olive oil and leave on the heat to allow the oil's flavour to emerge. Check the seasoning – this dish needs plenty of salt and pepper. In the last 5 minutes of cooking add your chosen herbs (if using). Serve with more oil drizzled on top if you like.

TURKISH SPICED BLACK-EYED PEAS
WITH YOGHURT & MINT BUTTER

In Turkey and the Middle East mint butter is often made with dried mint even when fresh leaves are available, but choose whichever you prefer.

FROM THE GROCER

80 ml (2½ fl oz/⅓ cup) olive oil

½ teaspoon ground cinnamon

2 teaspoons ground cumin

400 g (14 oz) tinned cherry tomatoes in thick juice

125 ml (4 fl oz/½ cup) chicken stock or water

2 teaspoons soft dark brown sugar

salt and freshly ground black pepper

800 g (1 lb 12 oz) tinned black-eyed peas, drained and rinsed

25 g (1 oz) unsalted butter

100 g (3½ oz) Greek-style yoghurt

FROM THE GREENGROCER

1 onion, chopped

4 garlic cloves, chopped

1 red chilli, halved, seeded and chopped

2 tablespoons chopped fresh mint or 2 teaspoons dried mint

Heat half the olive oil in a saucepan over a medium heat and add the onion. Cook until soft and golden, add the garlic and cook for 4 minutes or so. Add the chilli, cinnamon and cumin and cook for another 2 minutes. Tip in the tomatoes with their juice, the stock or water, sugar and salt and pepper. Bring to the boil, reduce the heat to a simmer and cook for about 20 minutes, stirring every so often. Add the black-eyed peas, stir well, season again and simmer for another 20 minutes. The mixture should be thick but add more stock or water if it gets too dry. The black-eyed peas shouldn't be falling apart.

Just before serving, heat the butter in a frying pan over a medium heat and add the mint, stirring briskly for about 15 seconds to release the fragrance. Remove from the heat.

Tip the black-eyed peas into a serving dish. Stir the yoghurt well so that it's not too firm and mix in the rest of the olive oil. Drizzle the yoghurt over the top of the beans and pour on the mint butter. Serve immediately.

crackers

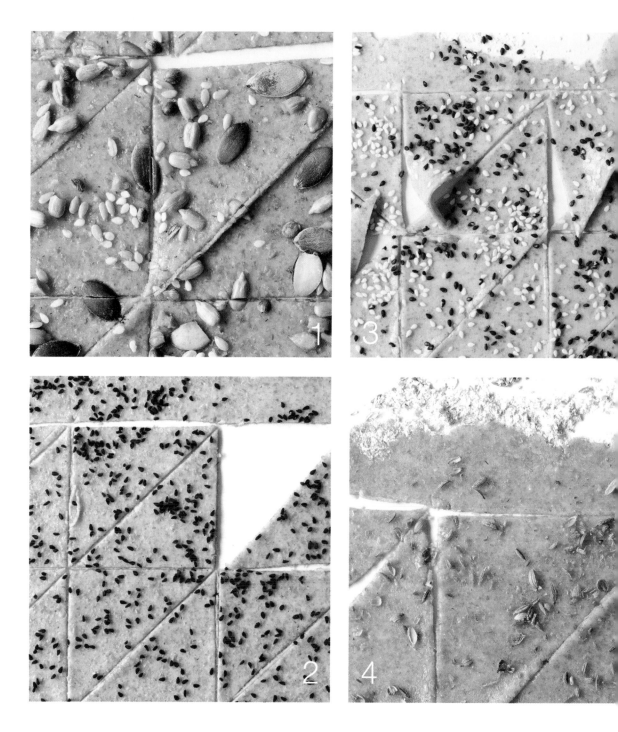

quick ideas

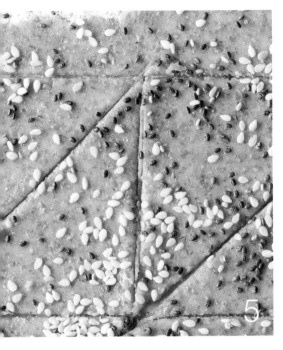

1. Basic wholemeal & seed crackers Process 200 g (7 oz/1⅓ cups) wholemeal (whole-wheat) flour, 1½ tablespoons soft light brown sugar, ½ teaspoon salt, 65 g (2¼ oz) butter and 80 ml (2½ fl oz/⅓ cup) water in a food processor to form a dough. On a floured surface, roll out to the thickness of stiff card. Brush with 1 lightly beaten egg white mixed with 1 tablespoon water and press 4 tablespoons mixed seeds into the dough. Cut into your desired cracker shapes and use a palette knife to lift each one onto a baking paper–lined baking tray. Cook for 25 minutes at 150°C (300°F). Increase the heat to 165°C (330°F) and cook for about 5 minutes more, or until just starting to brown.

2. Garlic & onion seed crackers Make the basic recipe but add 1 tablespoon garlic granules to the dough when kneading and sprinkle over 10 g (¼ oz) black onion seeds after brushing the dough with the egg wash.

3. Rye & sesame crackers Make the basic recipe but use half rye flour and half plain (all-purpose) flour. Sprinkle over 3 tablespoons white sesame seeds and 3 tablespoons black sesame seeds after brushing the dough with egg wash.

4. Spelt, coriander & cumin seed crackers Make the basic recipe using wholemeal (whole-wheat) spelt instead of wheat flour. Crush 2 tablespoons coriander seeds in a mortar, mix with 2 tablespoons cumin seeds and sprinkle the seeds over after brushing the dough with egg wash.

5. Buckwheat, chia & white sesame crackers Make the basic recipe using half wholegrain wheat flour and half buckwheat flour. Sprinkle with 4 tablespoons white sesame seeds and 2 tablespoons chia seeds after brushing the dough with egg wash.

6. Barley & caraway crackers Make the basic recipe using barley flour instead of wheat flour and sprinkle with 3 tablespoons caraway seeds after brushing the dough with egg wash.

TURKISH BARLEY & LENTIL SALAD
WITH TAHINI DRESSING

Barley, lentils and carrots may seem plain but this is a great dish in its own right, so consider serving it as a main course as well as a side dish. No meat is required – a bowl of Greek-style yoghurt is all you really need to go with it.

FROM THE GROCER

75 g (2¾ oz/⅓ cup) pearl barley

80 ml (2½ fl oz/⅓ cup) olive oil

½ teaspoon dried chilli flakes

2 teaspoons dried cumin

100 g (3½ oz) puy (tiny blue-green) lentils

2 tablespoons tomato passata (puréed tomatoes)

2 teaspoons soft light brown sugar

275 ml (9½ fl oz) vegetable stock or water

salt and freshly ground black pepper

105 ml (3½ fl oz) extra-virgin olive oil

150 g (5½ oz) plain yoghurt

150 g (5½ oz) tahini

FROM THE GREENGROCER

1 onion, roughly chopped

8 garlic cloves

6 large carrots, sliced into rounds about 4 mm (¼ in) thick

juice of 3 lemons

2 tablespoons roughly chopped flat-leaf (Italian) parsley

75 g (2¾ oz) rocket (arugula) leaves

Put the barley into a saucepan and cover with cold water. Bring to the boil, reduce the heat and cook until tender, about 30 minutes.

Meanwhile, heat the olive oil in a saucepan over a medium heat and sauté the onion until soft and golden. Finely chop 4 of the garlic cloves, add to the pan and cook for 2 minutes – don't let the garlic brown. Add the chilli flakes and cumin and cook for a further 2 minutes. Tip in the lentils, carrots, tomato passata, sugar and stock or water, and season with salt and pepper. Bring to the boil. Reduce the heat to a briskish simmer and cook until the carrots are soft and the lentils tender but not falling apart. The liquid should have been completely absorbed in that time but if you find it gets too dry add a little more.

In a large bowl, gently combine the lentil mixture with the barley, adding the juice of 1 lemon, 60 ml (2 fl oz/¼ cup) of the extra-virgin olive oil and the parsley. Taste for seasoning.

To make the dressing, beat the yoghurt into the tahini and add the remaining lemon juice, the remaining extra-virgin olive oil, the remaining garlic (crushed) and 80 ml (2½ fl oz/⅓ cup) water. Taste and season – it needs quite a lot of salt. You might also want to add a little more water or olive oil to thin the mixture.

Toss the rocket through the barley and lentil mixture and drizzle with some of the tahini dressing, serving the rest on the side.

INDIAN DAL
WITH CHILLI-FRIED ONIONS

This stalwart of many an Indian restaurant is a good, starchy dish to serve with more highly flavoured ones. It's even good on its own, just served with rice, as long as you have interesting chutneys alongside.

FROM THE GROCER

400 g (14 oz) split yellow mung beans

3 teaspoons ground turmeric

salt and freshly ground black pepper

2 tablespoons peanut oil

1½ teaspoons cumin seeds

1 teaspoon black mustard seeds

FROM THE GREENGROCER

6 garlic cloves, very finely chopped

4 cm (1½ in) piece of fresh ginger, finely chopped

1 green chilli, halved, seeded and finely chopped

½ small onion, thinly sliced

1 red chilli, halved, seeded and shredded

fresh coriander (cilantro) leaves, to serve

Wash the mung beans in a sieve until the water runs clear, transfer to a saucepan and cover with water. Bring to the boil, reduce the heat and add the garlic, ginger, turmeric and green chilli. Half cover the pan and cook over a very low heat for 1 hour 30 minutes, stirring from time to time. The mung beans should collapse into a purée. If you want a thinner purée add more water. If you want it thicker, remove the lid completely and cook until the mixture reduces to the consistency you like. Taste for seasoning.

Heat the peanut oil in a frying pan and cook the onion over a medium–low heat until soft. Increase the heat and fry until the onion darkens. Add the cumin seeds, mustard seeds and red chilli, and cook for another couple of minutes. Serve the mung beans with the onions on top and scattered with the coriander.

INDIAN RED LENTILS
WITH COCONUT

Spicy and slightly sweet, serve this as a side dish with meat or as a delicious main course with rice and a bowl of cucumber *raita*.

FROM THE GROCER
2 tablespoons sunflower oil

1 teaspoon ground turmeric

1 teaspoon ground cumin

1 tablespoon garam masala

250 g (9 oz/1 cup) red lentils

400 ml (14 fl oz) coconut milk

salt and freshly ground black pepper

FROM THE GREENGROCER
1 large onion, roughly chopped

2 cm (¾ in) piece of fresh ginger, finely chopped

4 garlic cloves, finely chopped

2 red chillies, halved, seeded and chopped

3 tablespoons roughly chopped coriander (cilantro) leaves

Heat the sunflower oil in a saucepan over a medium heat and sauté the onion until soft and golden. Add the ginger, garlic and chillies and cook for 2 minutes. Add the turmeric, cumin and garam masala, and cook for another 2 minutes.

Stir in the lentils and then cover with 600 ml (20½ fl oz) water. Bring to the boil, then reduce the heat and add the coconut milk. Season with salt and pepper. Gently simmer, stirring from time to time, until the lentils collapse into a purée, about 20–30 minutes depending on their age. Check the seasoning and stir in the coriander before serving, reserving a little to sprinkle on top.

SPICED RED LENTILS
WITH YOGHURT, CORIANDER & SESAME SEEDS

Feel free to add other vegetables to this – it's good with red capsicums (bell peppers) and eggplant (aubergine). Just sauté and add them to the pan before the lentils.

FROM THE GROCER

2 tablespoons olive oil

1½ teaspoons ground cumin

2 teaspoons ground coriander

200 g (7 oz) red lentils

300 ml (10 fl oz) water or
vegetable stock

400 g (14 oz) tinned chopped
tomatoes in thick juice

1½ tablespoons tomato passata
(puréed tomatoes)

salt and freshly ground black pepper

brown rice or burghul (bulgur wheat),
to serve

Greek-style yoghurt, to serve

1 tablespoon black sesame seeds,
to serve

FROM THE GREENGROCER

1 onion, roughly chopped

1 red capsicum (bell pepper), halved,
seeded and chopped

1 red chilli, halved, seeded and finely
chopped

a good squeeze of lemon

a generous handful of coriander
(cilantro) leaves, coarsely chopped

Heat the olive oil in a heavy-based saucepan and add the onion and capsicum. Cook over a medium–low heat, stirring a little, until soft, about 15 minutes. Add the cumin and ground coriander and cook for 2 minutes, stirring. Add the lentils, water or stock, tomatoes, tomato passata, salt and pepper, and chilli. Bring to the boil, then reduce the heat to a simmer and cook until the lentils have completely collapsed into a purée, about 25 minutes. Check every so often to make sure the mixture isn't drying out – you want to end up with a thick soupy mixture.

Taste for seasoning and stir in the squeeze of lemon juice and half the chopped coriander. Serve in bowls with brown rice or burghul, with a spoonful of Greek-style yoghurt on top. Sprinkle with the remaining chopped coriander and the sesame seeds.

SPRING COUSCOUS
WITH HERBS, LEMON & PISTACHIOS

Using the couscous as a base you can be as creative as you like with this, tossing other herbs or nuts into the mixture, orange zest instead of lemon, and even dried fruit or chopped tomatoes.

FROM THE GROCER

200 g (7 oz) wholemeal (whole-wheat) couscous

175 ml (6 fl oz) boiling water or chicken stock

90 ml (3 fl oz) extra-virgin olive oil

salt and freshly ground black pepper

25 g (¾ oz) unsalted pistachio nuts, chopped

FROM THE GREENGROCER

juice and zest of ½ lemon, removed in strips with a zester

1 spring onion (scallion), finely chopped

3 tablespoons each flat-leaf (Italian) parsley, mint and coriander (cilantro) leaves

Sprinkle the couscous into a shallow dish and add the water or stock and 2 tablespoons of the olive oil. Cover with plastic wrap and leave to plump up for about 15 minutes, then fork it to aerate and separate the grains. You can serve the couscous at this temperature or reheat it in the oven or microwave.

Stir in the remaining ingredients, taste for seasoning and serve.

ORANGE & PISTACHIO PILAFF

This is a beautiful looking dish and not an expensive one. In Iran, sautéed chicken and lamb are sometimes added to make a main course pilaff, and pulses can be thrown in too.

FROM THE GROCER

300 g (10½ oz/1½ cups) brown basmati rice

900 ml (30½ fl oz) chicken stock

40 g (1½ oz) butter

2 teaspoons caster (superfine) sugar

25 g (1 oz) unsalted pistachio nuts or blanched almonds, chopped

FROM THE GREENGROCER

1 orange

1 onion, finely chopped

2 garlic cloves, finely chopped

125 g (4½ oz) carrots, cut into matchsticks

3 tablespoons chopped coriander (cilantro) leaves

Place the rice in a sieve and rinse under running water until the water runs clear. Remove the rind from half the orange in broad strips. Slice away as much of the white pith as possible and cut the rind into fine julienne strips. Squeeze the juice from the orange and add to the stock.

Heat 15 g (½ oz) of the butter in a heavy-based saucepan over a medium heat and sauté the onion until soft and pale gold. Add the garlic and cook for another couple of minutes. Stir the rice into the buttery juices and cook until just beginning to toast. Add 600 ml (20½ fl oz) of the stock mixture and bring to the boil. When the rice starts to look pitted, reduce the heat to very low and cover so it can steam. Top up with more stock every so often and fork occasionally so the rice does not stick to the bottom of the pan. The rice should cook in about 40 minutes. Brown rice never softens as much as white rice – it will still be a little firm in the centre and 'nutty'.

While the rice is cooking, melt the rest of the butter in a saucepan and sauté the carrots over a medium heat until they soften a little. Remove the carrots and set aside, add the orange rind and cook over medium heat until it softens a little – it will only take a couple of minutes. Add the sugar and stir until the moisture is cooked off and the rind is slightly caramelised. Gently fork this into the rice along with the carrots, nuts and coriander. Serve immediately.

WARM BARLEY
WITH ROAST PUMPKIN & FETA

If feta cheese seems slightly summery for this good autumnal dish, add shaved gruyère or crumbled gorgonzola instead. If you do, change the herb to parsley. You could also add toasted hazelnuts and dress with nut oil rather than olive oil.

FROM THE GROCER

60 ml (2 fl oz/¼ cup) olive oil

salt and freshly ground black pepper

150 g (5½ oz) pearl barley

2 tablespoons extra-virgin olive oil

1 tablespoon white balsamic vinegar

1 tablespoon pumpkin seeds (pepitas), lightly toasted

100 g (3½ oz/⅔ cup) crumbled feta cheese (preferably barrel-aged)

FROM THE GREENGROCER

750 g (1 lb 11 oz) pumpkin (winter squash) or butternut pumpkin (squash), peeled, seeded and cut into chunks

2 garlic cloves, finely sliced

3 tablespoons roughly chopped coriander (cilantro) leaves

Preheat the oven to 200°C (400°F). Scatter the pumpkin in a roasting tin, add 2 tablespoons of the olive oil and season with salt and pepper. Toss together with your hands to make sure each piece is coated in oil. Roast for 20–30 minutes. The pumpkin should be completely tender and a little singed in places. About 10 minutes before the end of cooking, take the roasting tin out of the oven, scatter the garlic over the pumpkin, add the rest of the olive oil and return to the oven.

While the pumpkin is cooking, put the barley into a saucepan and cover with plenty of cold water. Bring to the boil, reduce the heat and cook until tender, about 30 minutes. Drain, rinse with boiling water, shake dry and immediately mix with the extra-virgin olive oil, vinegar and seasoning. Stir in the coriander and pumpkin seeds and gently fork through the pumpkin and the feta. This is best served warm or at room temperature.

SALAD OF SPELT, AUTUMN LEAVES, NUTS & BLACK GRAPES

To turn this perfect autumnal salad into a main course, toss in nuggets of goat's cheese or blue cheese.

FROM THE GROCER

1 tablespoon white balsamic vinegar

80 ml (2½ fl oz/⅓ cup) hazelnut or walnut oil

2½ tablespoons fruity extra-virgin olive oil

1 teaspoon crème de cassis

salt and freshly ground black pepper

150 g (5½ oz) spelt

15 g (½ oz) toasted hazelnuts or walnuts, very roughly chopped

FROM THE GREENGROCER

1 head of red chicory (radicchio), leaves separated

75 g (2¾ oz/2½ cups) watercress, thick stalks removed

50 g (1¾ oz) small black seedless grapes, halved if large

To make the dressing, whisk together the vinegar, hazelnut or walnut oil, the extra-virgin olive oil, crème de cassis and salt and pepper. Set aside.

Put the spelt into a saucepan, cover with cold water and bring to the boil. Reduce the heat to a simmer and cook for 25 minutes. The spelt should be soft but still have a little bite. Drain, season and dress with about half of the dressing and leave to cool a little. Taste for seasoning – spelt can take quite a bit. When it has cooled to room temperature, gently toss with the chicory, watercress, grapes and nuts, and remaining dressing, if desired. Serve immediately.

SPELT, FIG & POMEGRANATE SALAD

If your figs aren't quite ripe, cook them in a chargrill pan and drizzle with a little honey before tossing into the salad. This is excellent on the side with pork or lamb.

FROM THE GROCER

150 g (5½ oz) spelt

1½ tablespoons extra-virgin olive oil

2 teaspoons white balsamic vinegar

salt and freshly ground black pepper

FROM THE GREENGROCER

¼ small red onion, sliced wafer-thin

2 tablespoons roughly chopped
flat-leaf (Italian) parsley

1 tablespoon chopped mint

8 fresh ripe figs, tips snipped off,
halved or quartered depending
on size

seeds from ½ pomegranate

Put the spelt into a saucepan and cover with plenty of cold water. Bring to the boil, reduce the heat and cook until tender, about 30 minutes. Drain and immediately mix with the olive oil, vinegar and salt and pepper. Stir in the onion and herbs. Season the cut side of each fig with salt and pepper and gently toss into the spelt. Add the pomegranate seeds just before serving as they tend to bleed their juice.

PEA, RADISH & FARRO SALAD

Light and summery, this salad is well behaved enough to make in advance.

FROM THE GROCER
250 g (9 oz) farro
a dash of dijon mustard
½ teaspoon caster (superfine) sugar
75 ml (2½ fl oz) extra-virgin olive oil
salt and freshly ground black pepper

FROM THE GREENGROCER
juice of ½ lemon
150 g (5½ oz) peas (podded weight)
150 g (5½ oz) French breakfast radishes
½ red onion, very finely sliced
8 mint sprigs, leaves torn

FROM THE BAKER
seeded rolls, to serve (optional)

Put the farro into a saucepan and add enough water to come about 3 cm (1¼ in) above the level of the grains. Bring to the boil, reduce the heat and simmer for 20–30 minutes, or until the grains are tender but retain a little bite. Try not to stir the farro while it's cooking, as you don't want to release the starch. The liquid will be absorbed but if the farro gets too dry add a little more water.

Once the farro is done, drain off any remaining liquid. Mix together the lemon juice, mustard, sugar, olive oil and salt and pepper and pour over the farro. Gently fork the dressing through and leave to cool.

Cook the peas in lightly salted boiling water until just tender. Drain. Trim the radishes and slice them wafer-thin lengthways so that you are left with little tear-shaped slices. When the farro has cooled, gently toss through the peas, radishes, onion and mint. Season really well as farro is starchy. It also soaks up dressing so you may need to add more olive oil or lemon juice for the texture as much as for the taste. If you add more dressing, adjust the seasoning again. Serve with seeded rolls (if desired).

sweet things

BLACKBERRY, APPLE & MAPLE BROWN BETTY

This is a great homely American dessert. If you don't like the flavour of maple syrup leave it out and add an extra 40 g (1½ oz) of soft light brown sugar.

FROM THE GROCER

150 g (5½ oz) soft light brown sugar

3 tablespoons sunflower kernels

½ teaspoon ground mixed (pumpkin pie) spice

½ teaspoon ground ginger

250 g (9 oz) stale brown bread, torn into little chunks

100 g (3½ oz) butter, melted, plus extra for greasing

25 ml (¾ fl oz) maple syrup

whipped cream or vanilla ice cream, to serve (optional)

FROM THE GREENGROCER

2 cooking apples, peeled and cored

500 g (1 lb 2 oz) blackberries

Preheat the oven to 180°C (350°F). Mix the sugar, sunflower kernels and spices together. Place the torn bread into a medium bowl and add 3 tablespoons of the sugar and spice mixture. Pour over the melted butter and mix well.

Slice the apples thinly and mix with the blackberries and the rest of the sugar and spice mixture.

Grease a 750 ml (25½ fl oz/3 cup) capacity gratin or pie dish and pile in half the bread mixture. Scatter the apples and blackberries on top and pour over the maple syrup. Add the rest of the bread mixture, loosely cover with foil and bake for 20 minutes. Remove the foil and bake for a further 20 minutes, or until the fruit is tender and the top golden.

Serve with whipped cream or vanilla ice cream.

CRANBERRY, APPLE & OAT CRUMBLE

Cranberries are great in crumbles. This one is nice and tart – and just the right side of healthy. Change the nuts if you like, but pecans are suitably American.

FROM THE GROCER

200 g (7 oz) soft light brown sugar

a generous glug of crème de cassis or crème de mure (optional)

75 g (2¾ oz/½ cup) plain (all-purpose) flour

75 g (2¾ oz/½ cup) wholemeal (whole-wheat) flour

175 g (6 oz) cold butter, cut into cubes

150 g (5½ oz) soft dark brown sugar

50 g (1¾ oz/½ cup) brown breadcrumbs

50 g (1¾ oz/½ cup) rolled (porridge) oats

50 g (1¾ oz/½ cup) pecans, very roughly chopped

crème fraîche or sweetened whipped cream, to serve (optional)

FROM THE GREENGROCER

300 g (10½ oz) cranberries

700 g (1 lb 9 oz) cooking apples, peeled, cored and chopped

Preheat the oven to 180°C (350°F). Put the cranberries into a saucepan with 80 ml (2½ fl oz/⅓ cup) water. Bring to the boil, reduce the heat and cook until the berries are just bursting. Don't be tempted to add any more water or the mixture will be too wet.

Put the apples and cranberries into a 2 litre (68 fl oz/8 cup) capacity pie dish and add the soft light brown sugar. Mix to make sure all the fruit gets coated in sugar and drizzle over the alcohol (if using).

In a food processor, pulse together the flours, butter and soft dark brown sugar until the mixture looks like breadcrumbs. Transfer to a bowl and stir through the brown breadcrumbs, oats and pecans. Pat this mixture on top of the fruit and bake for 35–40 minutes. The fruit should be completely tender and the top brown and bubbling. Serve with crème fraîche or sweetened whipped cream (if using).

BROWN RICE PUDDING
WITH DRIED FRUIT IN VERJUICE & HONEY

Rice pudding made partly with brown short-grain rice is chewier and nuttier than regular rice pudding – it has a lovely texture and flavour that works very well with dried fruit and makes a good autumn dessert.

FROM THE GROCER

600 ml (20½ fl oz) verjuice

80 ml (2½ fl oz/⅓ cup) runny honey

40 g (1½ oz) caster (superfine) sugar

4 dried bay leaves

150 g (5½ oz) muscatel raisins, on the stalk if possible

175 g (6 oz) dried apricots

100 g (3½ oz) brown short-grain rice

50 g (1¾ oz) white pudding rice or white short-grain rice

500 ml (17 fl oz/2 cups) full-cream (whole) milk, plus extra to taste

4 tablespoons soft light brown sugar

50–75 ml (1¾–2½ fl oz) thick (double-heavy) cream (optional)

chopped pistachio nuts, to serve

FROM THE GREENGROCER

2 broad strips of lemon rind

Put the verjuice, honey, caster sugar, lemon rind and bay leaves into a saucepan and bring to the boil, stirring a little to help the sugar dissolve. Add the raisins to the pan, along with the apricots. If you have long stalks of muscatel raisins, snip them in half first. Cook the fruit gently for about 25 minutes, remove from the heat and leave to plump up – a couple of hours is fine but 24 hours is best. Remove the bay leaves and lemon rind.

Put the brown rice into a heavy-based saucepan and cover with water. Bring to the boil, reduce the heat to a brisk simmer and cook for 20 minutes, or until the rice starts to soften. Drain and place in a saucepan with the white pudding rice, milk and soft light brown sugar. Bring to the boil, reduce the heat to very low and cook for about 40 minutes, stirring regularly and keeping an eye on the milk level. Eventually you will have soft creamy rice speckled with the brown, nuttier grains. You can serve the rice now or leave it to cool. If you leave it to cool it will thicken so you may need to add more milk to loosen the mixture. It also benefits from a good slosh of cream if you want something a little richer. Serve with the fruit and scatter the top with pistachio nuts.

PEASANT GIRLS IN A MIST

A Scandinavian pudding: in the summer you can make it with redcurrants (just shake them in plenty of sugar and leave them sitting for an hour – there's no need to cook them) or poached rhubarb.

FROM THE GROCER

4 tablespoons soft light brown sugar, plus extra for sweetening (optional)

25 g (1 oz) unsalted butter

100 g (3½ oz) coarse rye or pumpernickel breadcrumbs

50 g (1¾ oz) soft dark brown sugar, plus extra for sprinkling (optional)

½ teaspoon ground cinnamon

¼ teaspoon ground cloves

300 ml (10½ fl oz) thick (double/heavy) cream

4 tablespoons icing (confectioners') sugar

1½ teaspoons aquavit or vodka, or to taste

3 tablespoons toasted hazelnuts, roughly chopped

FROM THE GREENGROCER

2 bramley apples, peeled and cored

Cut the apples into chunks and put in a saucepan with the soft light brown sugar and 2 tablespoons water. Cook over a low heat, stirring from time to time and mashing a little to help break up the apples. You want the apples to be completely soft. Don't be tempted to add more water – the apples will start releasing their own juice. Taste for sweetness, adding a little extra sugar if necessary, and transfer to a bowl to cool.

Melt the butter in a frying pan and add the breadcrumbs and soft dark brown sugar. Sauté, stirring, over a medium heat until the breadcrumbs are toasted and lightly caramelised. Stir in the cinnamon and cloves and cook for another minute. Tip onto a plate and leave to cool completely.

Whip the cream and add the icing sugar and aquavit or vodka.

Have your components – apples, breadcrumbs and cream – ready to layer up in a glass serving bowl, or you can do single servings in glasses or flat soup bowls. Start with the apples, then breadcrumbs, then cream. Repeat until you have used up the components, ending with the hazelnuts on top. You can sprinkle a little more dark brown sugar on top too – it sinks into the cream and makes a lovely dark, toffee-ish topping. You can eat this immediately or keep it in the refrigerator, covered, until you want to serve it. Let it warm up a little at room temperature if you chill it, otherwise the cream can be too firm.

POMMES LORRAINES

A healthy and easy pudding from the Alsace region of France. Try it after a wintry Sunday lunch.

FROM THE GROCER

150 g (5½ oz) raisins

225 ml (7½ fl oz) orange juice or apple cider

80 g (2¾ oz) butter, plus extra for greasing

125 g (4½ oz/⅔ cup, lightly packed) soft light brown sugar

150 g (5½ oz/1½ cups) wholemeal (whole-wheat) breadcrumbs

whipped cream or crème fraîche, to serve

FROM THE GREENGROCER

grated zest of 1 orange

1 kg (2 lb 3 oz) tart eating apples

Preheat the oven to 180°C (350°F). Put the raisins and orange juice or cider in a small saucepan and bring to the boil. Reduce the heat and simmer gently for about 7 minutes. Remove from the heat. Add the orange zest and leave to stand for about 15 minutes so the raisins can plump up.

Grease a 1 litre (34 fl oz/4 cup) capacity baking dish with butter. Peel, halve, core and thinly slice the apples and arrange them in a layer in the dish. Sprinkle over some of the sugar and spoon on some of the raisins and their liquid. Next, add a layer of breadcrumbs then dot with some of the butter. Repeat until all the ingredients are used, finishing with a layer of breadcrumbs and butter.

Bake for 40 minutes, or until the apples are tender – test with a skewer – and the top is golden. Leave to cool slightly and serve with whipped cream or crème fraîche.

PEAR & EAU DE VIE CLAFOUTIS

You really need perfectly ripe pears for this. If you can't find them you will need to poach or sauté the pear slices in a sugar syrup or butter until tender before you begin.

FROM THE GROCER

80 ml (2½ fl oz/⅓ cup) pear eau de vie

150 ml (5 fl oz) full-cream (whole) milk

150 ml (5 fl oz) thick (double/heavy) cream

1 teaspoon natural vanilla extract

25 g (1 oz) unsalted butter, plus extra for greasing

3 eggs

125 g (4½ oz) caster (superfine) sugar

a pinch of salt

50 g (1¾ oz/⅓ cup) wholemeal (whole-wheat) flour

15 g (½ oz) crushed hazelnuts or flaked almonds

icing (confectioners') sugar, to serve

whipped cream, to serve (optional)

FROM THE GREENGROCER

3 ripe pears

Preheat the oven to 180°C (350°F). Halve and core the pears, then cut each half lengthways into slices. Immediately place the slices in a bowl and cover with the eau de vie, turning the fruit to coat well.

Mix the milk, cream and vanilla together. Generously grease a shallow gratin dish with butter – a metal or cast-iron dish with a capacity of 1.2 litres (41 fl oz) is best – and arrange the pear slices in the bottom. Mix the alcohol that the pears have been soaking in into the milk and cream.

Whisk the eggs, sugar and salt together until the mixture triples in volume and is pale and fluffy. You really need a powerful beater for this. Fold in the flour and then the milk and cream mixture. Pour the batter over the pear slices. Dot the butter over the surface. Bake for 30 minutes, or until the batter is set – stick a skewer into the middle and it will come out clean if ready.

Scatter over the nuts about 5 minutes before the end of cooking.
Sift a little icing sugar over the top before serving with whipped cream (if using).

PLUM & GRANOLA YOGHURT POTS

This is healthy but not austere so you won't even notice you're eating something that's also good for you.

FROM THE GROCER

sunflower oil, for greasing

125 g (4½ oz) caster (superfine) sugar

1½ tablespoons white sesame seeds

2 star anise

150 g (5½ oz) soft light brown sugar

75 ml (2½ fl oz) orange juice

300 g (10½ oz) Greek-style yoghurt

50 ml (1¾ fl oz) thick (double-heavy) cream

½ teaspoon natural vanilla extract

50 g (1¾ oz) icing (confectioners') sugar, or to taste

250 g (9 oz) granola (see page 28)

FROM THE GREENGROCER

12 unripe plums, halved and stoned

2.5 cm (1 in) piece of fresh ginger, peeled and finely grated

Grease a baking tray with sunflower oil. Put the caster sugar and 2 tablespoons water into a saucepan over a low heat. Gently heat until the sugar has completely dissolved. Increase the heat and boil the mixture until it turns to caramel. Add the sesame seeds and immediately pour onto the baking tray. Leave to set. When the caramel has hardened, break it into large shards.

Preheat the oven to 180°C (350°F). Put the plums in a bowl with the ginger, star anise and soft light brown sugar, and mix everything together with your hands. Place the plums in an ovenproof dish large enough to take them in a single layer. Pour the orange juice into the dish and bake for 20–25 minutes, depending on the ripeness of the plums. If the juice left in the dish is thick and syrupy, leave to cool. If there's a lot of thin juice left, remove the plums with a slotted spoon, pour the juice into a saucepan and boil to reduce and thicken. You should end up with about 125 ml (4 fl oz/½ cup) of liquid; it will thicken more as it cools. When cool, pour it back over the plums.

Mix the yoghurt with the cream, vanilla and icing sugar. Have everything ready to assemble in 125–150 ml (4–5 fl oz) glasses. Layer the components in each glass starting with some plums, then some yoghurt, then a layer of granola. Repeat. Stick a caramel shard in the top before serving.

BROWN BREAD ICE CREAM

Use brown bread with oats and seeds if you can find it.

FROM THE GROCER

20 g (¾ oz) unsalted butter

75 g (2¾ oz/¾ cup) brown breadcrumbs

50 g (1¾ oz) soft dark brown sugar

500 ml (17 fl oz/2 cups) thickened (whipping) cream

75 g (2¾ oz) soft light brown sugar

½ teaspoon natural vanilla extract

60 ml (2 fl oz/¼ cup) dark rum

FROM THE GREENGROCER

blueberries, to serve

Melt the butter in a frying pan and add the breadcrumbs. Sauté until golden, stirring often, then add the soft dark brown sugar, pressing with the back of a wooden spoon to break down any lumps. Continue to sauté, stirring, until the sugar has caramelised the breadcrumbs. Be very careful not to burn the mixture. Scatter onto a baking tray and leave to cool. If the mixture cools into clumps break them into little bits.

Whip the cream until loose peaks form, adding the soft light brown sugar as you go. Add the vanilla and rum and stir in the caramelised breadcrumbs. Spoon into a broad shallow container and freeze – this ice cream doesn't need to be churned. Serve with blueberries. You can, if you want to, sauté more crumbs in butter and sugar and scatter them over the top so that you have cold ice cream and warm crumbs.

NORTHERN ITALIAN BUCKWHEAT CAKE

This cake is surprisingly light and great at teatime with a good strong espresso. Replace the berry filling with jam if you like, but one that isn't too sweet.

FROM THE GROCER

350 g (12½ oz) caster (superfine) sugar

250 g (9 oz) butter, at room temperature, plus extra for greasing

6 large eggs, separated, at room temperature

250 g (9 oz) buckwheat flour

1½ tablespoons baking powder

a good pinch of salt

1 teaspoon ground cinnamon

125 g (4½ oz) almonds, hazelnuts or walnuts, very finely ground

300 g (10½ oz) frozen berries such as raspberries, blackberries or blackcurrants, or a mixture

150 g (5½ oz) dried sour cherries or cranberries

200 ml (7 fl oz) red wine or water

5 cm (2 in) piece of cinnamon stick (optional)

175 g (6 oz) crème fraîche

150 g (5½ oz) mascarpone

1½ tablespoons icing (confectioners') sugar, plus extra for dusting

FROM THE GREENGROCER

finely grated zest of 1 lemon

Preheat the oven to 180°C (350°F). Cream together 150 g (5½ oz) of the caster sugar with the butter until pale and fluffy. Add the lemon zest and then the egg yolks one at a time, mixing well after each addition. Fold in the flour, baking powder, salt, ground cinnamon and ground nuts.

Beat the egg whites until they form soft peaks. Whisk in 50 g (1¾ oz) of the caster sugar and fold in another 50 g (1¾ oz) of the caster sugar with a spoon. Fold the egg whites into the flour mixture using a large metal spoon, trying not to knock the air out while mixing thoroughly.

Grease two 20 cm (8 in) round springform cake tins with butter and line the bases with baking paper. Spoon equal amounts of batter into each tin and bake for 30–40 minutes. Test for doneness by inserting a skewer into the middle of each cake; it should come out clean.

Meanwhile, put the berries, dried fruit, red wine or water, the remaining caster sugar and cinnamon stick (if using) in a medium saucepan and bring to the boil, stirring to dissolve the sugar. Boil for about 8 minutes. The syrup should be thick and will thicken more as it cools. Remove the cinnamon stick (if used) and scrape the berries and syrup into a bowl to cool. In a separate bowl, mix together the crème fraîche, mascarpone and icing sugar.

When the cakes are ready, turn them onto a wire rack. When completely cool spread the mascarpone mixture over the top of one cake and spread the syrup on top. Put the other cake on top and dust generously with icing sugar.

MOST kinds of raw seeds can be used here to make smooth and delicious milk – try sesame seeds, sunflower kernels, hemp seeds, linseeds (flax seeds), pumpkin seeds (pepitas) or poppy seeds, but make sure they are not roasted.

how to
MAKE SEED MILK

1 Put 100 g (3½ oz) seeds in a bowl and completely cover with cold water. Leave to soak overnight. The seeds will get much softer in that time.

2 Drain the seeds and put them in a blender with 450 ml (15 fl oz) warm water. Blend on a high speed until the mixture is smooth.

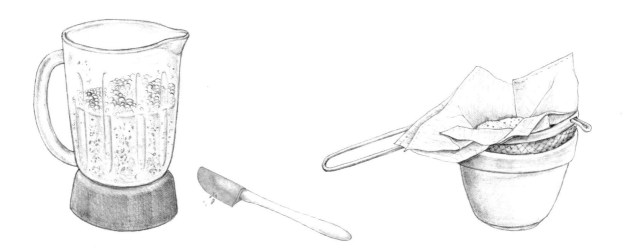

3 You will have to keep stopping the blender to scrape down the sides and around the blade. You can add a little more warm water if you need to help the blending along.

4 Pour the contents of the blender into a sieve lined with a double layer of muslin (cheesecloth) or a brand new perforated kitchen wash cloth, set over a bowl. The seed milk will start to run through.

5 To help extract as much milk as possible, pick the cloth up to form a 'bag' and squeeze tight. Keep squeezing until you are just left with dry pulp in the cloth.

6 Sweeten the milk with soft light brown sugar, honey or maple syrup and process again in a clean blender. To flavour, add ½ cinnamon stick, ½ vanilla bean or the crushed seeds of 4 cardamom pods, and heat in a saucepan until warm. Leave to allow the flavourings to infuse the milk for 30 minutes before straining. Makes about 400 ml (13½ fl oz).

SO-GOOD-FOR-YOU BANANA CAKE

It is crucial that the bananas you use for this are so ripe that their skins are almost black – it makes a huge difference to both the taste and the texture.

FROM THE GROCER

115 g (4 oz) butter, at room temperature, plus extra for greasing

160 g (5½ oz) soft light brown sugar

1 teaspoon natural vanilla extract

2 eggs, lightly beaten

3 tablespoons plain yoghurt

100 g (3½ oz/⅔ cup) plain (all-purpose) flour

100 g (3½ oz/⅔ cup) malthouse bread flour

1 teaspoon baking powder

½ teaspoon bicarbonate of soda (baking soda)

100 g (3½ oz/1 cup) pecans, toasted and chopped

2 tablespoons sunflower kernels

1 tablespoon linseeds (flax seeds)

icing (confectioners') sugar, for dusting (optional)

FROM THE GREENGROCER

finely grated zest of 1 orange

3 very ripe bananas

Preheat the oven to 180°C (350°F). Grease a 23 x 13 cm (9 x 5 in) loaf (bar) tin with butter and line the base with baking paper.

Beat the butter and sugar together until light and fluffy. Mix in the orange zest and vanilla and then beat in the eggs a little at a time. The mixture will look curdled but don't worry – it will come together when you add the flour.

Mash the bananas, getting rid of as many lumps as possible, and stir them into the butter and egg mixture followed by the yoghurt. Fold in the flours with the baking powder, bicarbonate of soda and three-quarters of the nuts and seeds. Be careful not to over-mix. Spoon the batter into the prepared loaf tin, sprinkle the remaining seeds on top and bake for 1 hour. The cake should have risen and a skewer inserted into the middle should come out clean. If the nuts and seeds are browning too much put some foil over the top.

Leave the cake in the tin to cool for 5 minutes and then run a knife along each side to loosen it before turning out onto a wire rack. Peel off the paper and leave to cool completely before carefully turning it the right way up. You can sift a light dusting of icing sugar over the top or just leave it as it is. Wrap in foil to keep moist. The cake will keep well for up to 4 days.

ANZAC BISCUITS

These are the simplest biscuits (cookies) you can make – it's just melt and mix – and everyone seems to love them. If you don't like coconut, just replace it with more oats. You can also add seeds.

FROM THE GROCER

115 g (4 oz) butter, at room temperature

55 g (2 oz/¼ cup) golden caster (superfine) sugar or soft light brown sugar

2 tablespoons golden syrup (light corn syrup)

½ teaspoon bicarbonate of soda (baking soda)

70 g (2½ oz) plain (all-purpose) flour

a pinch of salt

100 g (3½ oz/1 cup) rolled (porridge) oats

60 g (2 oz/⅔ cup) desiccated (shredded) coconut

Preheat the oven to 170°C (340°F). Line baking trays – you will probably need two or three unless they are very big – with baking paper.

Heat the butter, sugar and golden syrup together in a saucepan over a low heat. When everything is melted together, remove from the heat. Dissolve the bicarbonate of soda in 1 tablespoon hot water and add this to the butter mixture. Stir in the dry ingredients and mix to form a dough.

Place teaspoonfuls of the dough onto the prepared baking trays, leaving a good 5 cm (2 in) gap between them, as the biscuits will spread out as they cook. Bake for 12–15 minutes – they should be golden. They will crisp up while they cool so don't try to move them as soon as they come out of the oven.

GLAZED UPSIDE DOWN APRICOT & HAZELNUT CAKE

You can replace the apricots with plums, and glaze the top with plum jam or redcurrant jelly.

FROM THE GROCER

200 g (7 oz) butter, plus extra
for greasing

125 g (4½ oz) caster (superfine)
sugar

20–24 shelled hazelnuts

150 g (5½ oz) soft light brown sugar

2 eggs, beaten

1 teaspoon natural vanilla extract

50 g (1¾ oz/⅓ cup) plain
(all-purpose) flour

50 g (1¾ oz/⅓ cup) wholemeal
(whole-wheat) flour

1½ teaspoons baking powder

100 g (3½ oz) ground hazelnuts

125 ml (4 fl oz/½ cup) full-cream
(whole) milk

4 tablespoons apricot jam

crème fraîche, sweetened Greek-
style yoghurt or sweetened whipped
cream, to serve (optional)

FROM THE GREENGROCER

10–12 fresh apricots (not too ripe),
halved and stoned

Preheat the oven to 180°C (350°F). Grease a 23–25 cm (9–10 in) round cake tin with butter.

Put the caster sugar and 75 ml (2½ fl oz) water into a small saucepan and bring to the boil, stirring as the sugar dissolves. Boil until the mixture caramelises. Remove the pan from the heat and add 50 g (1¾ oz) of the butter – be careful, as the mixture will splutter – and stir. Pour into the prepared tin. Put a shelled hazelnut into the cavity of each apricot half and place the apricots close together, cut side down, on the caramel.

Cream the rest of the butter and the soft light brown sugar together until light and fluffy. Add the beaten eggs a little at a time, then the vanilla. In a separate bowl, sift the flours and baking powder together and put the bran from the flour in the sieve back into the mixture. Add the ground hazelnuts. With the beaters on low, add the flour mixture to the batter, alternating with the milk.

Spoon the mixture over the apricots and bake for 50 minutes, or until a skewer inserted in the middle comes out clean. Leave for about 2 minutes, then run a knife between the tin and the side of the cake. Invert onto a plate. Ease off any stuck apricots and put them on top of the cake.

Heat the jam in a small saucepan with 1 tablespoon water. Bring to the boil, then reduce the heat and simmer until thickened, about 1 minute. Push through a sieve and leave to cool. Thickly brush the top of the cake with the jam. Serve cold with crème fraîche, sweetened Greek-style yoghurt or sweetened whipped cream.

CHOCOLATE & BROWN SUGAR CAKE

A very good cake for children, this is reasonably healthy and quick to make and ice. It keeps well un-iced if you want to make it a few days in advance of serving.

FROM THE GROCER

150 g (5½ oz) butter, at room temperature, plus extra for greasing

225 g (8 oz/1½ cups) self-raising wholemeal (whole-wheat) flour

50 g (1¾ oz) unsweetened (Dutch) cocoa powder

¼ teaspoon bicarbonate of soda (baking soda)

175 g (6 oz) soft dark brown sugar

2 eggs, lightly beaten

250 g (9 oz/1 cup) plain yoghurt

35 ml (1¼ fl oz) milk, plus a little more if necessary

225 g (8 oz) dark chocolate, broken into small pieces

15 g (½ oz) unsalted butter

100 g (3½ oz) crème fraîche

Preheat the oven to 180°C (350°F). Grease a 20 cm (8 in) square cake tin with butter and line the base with baking paper.

Sift the flour, cocoa powder and bicarbonate of soda into a bowl. Put the bran that collects in the sieve back into the mixture.

Beat the butter and sugar together until fluffy and light and then add the eggs a little at a time, beating well after each addition. Stir in the yoghurt and fold in the flour mixture. Add enough milk to produce a reluctant dropping consistency. Scrape the batter into the prepared tin and bake for about 35 minutes. You can test to see whether it's done by sticking a skewer into the middle – it should come out clean. Leave the cake in the tin for 10 minutes, then turn out onto a wire rack to cool completely.

To make the glaze, melt the chocolate in a bowl set over a saucepan of simmering water. Stir a little to help it along but be careful not to let the chocolate get too hot – the bottom of the bowl should not touch the water. Remove the bowl from the heat, add the unsalted butter and stir until completely melted. Add the crème fraîche and stir vigorously. Leave to cool and firm up a little before you spread the glaze over the cake with a palette knife. Leave to set before cutting.

SUPER SEEDED CARROT CAKE

This is a particularly good carrot cake packed with seeds and made with wholegrain flours.

FROM THE GROCER

150 g (5½ oz) raisins

80 ml (2½ fl oz/⅓ cup) apple juice

butter, for greasing

115 g (4 oz) self-raising wholemeal (whole-wheat) flour

115 g (4 oz) wholemeal (whole-wheat) spelt flour

1¼ teaspoons baking powder

1 teaspoon bicarbonate of soda (baking soda)

1 teaspoon mixed (pumpkin pie) spice

2 eggs

150 g (5½ oz) soft light brown sugar

125 ml (4 fl oz/½ cup) sunflower oil

50 g (1¾ oz/½ cup) pecans, chopped

25 g (1 oz) sunflower kernels

2 tablespoons pumpkin seeds (pepitas), roughly chopped

1½ tablespoons chia seeds

1½ tablespoons linseeds (flax seeds)

200 g (7 oz) cream cheese

3 tablespoons icing (confectioners') sugar

FROM THE GREENGROCER

275 g (9½ oz) peeled carrot, grated

finely grated zest of 1 orange

finely grated zest of 1 lemon

Put the raisins into a small saucepan and cover with the apple juice. Bring to the boil, then let the raisins soak for about 30 minutes until they are nicely plump.

Preheat the oven to 160°C (320°F). Grease a 23 cm (9 in) square cake tin with butter and line the base with baking paper. In a large bowl, mix together both flours, the baking powder, bicarbonate of soda and mixed spice.

Beat the eggs and sugar together for about 2 minutes until foamy, then add the sunflower oil. Fold the dry ingredients into the egg mixture, then stir in the raisins with their soaking juice, the carrot, citrus zest, pecans, all of the sunflower kernels and 1 tablespoon each of the pumpkin and chia seeds and linseeds. Mix well – the batter will be quite stiff.

Scrape the batter into the prepared tin and bake for 1 hour. A skewer inserted into the middle should come out clean when done. Leave to stand for 10 minutes, then turn out onto a wire rack to cool for 15 minutes. Peel the paper off and turn the cake the right way up. Allow to cool completely before adding the topping.

To make the topping, beat the cream cheese with a wooden spoon and add the icing sugar. Put in the refrigerator to firm up a little, then spread the topping over the cake. Scatter with the remaining seeds and cut into 16 squares.

APPLE & POLENTA CAKE

This is an incredibly easy Italian cake similar to the French dessert clafoutis – a dessert cake rather than a cake to eat for afternoon tea.

FROM THE GROCER

100 g (3½ oz) dried figs

100 g (3½ oz) dried sour cherries

butter, for greasing

100 g (3½ oz/⅔ cup) polenta

130 g (4½ oz) plain (all-purpose) flour

100 g (3½ oz/1 cup) ground almonds

100 g (3½ oz/1 cup) breadcrumbs

a pinch of salt

100 g (3½ oz) soft light brown sugar

3 eggs

500 ml (17 fl oz/2 cups) milk

100 g (3½ oz) honey

55 ml (1¾ fl oz) olive oil

1 tablespoon orange-blossom water

icing (confectioners') sugar, for dusting

crème fraîche or whipped cream, to serve (optional)

FROM THE GREENGROCER

500 g (1 lb 2 oz) eating apples

juice of ½ lemon

zest of 2 lemons

zest of 1 orange

Put the figs and cherries in a bowl and cover with just-boiled water. Leave to soak for 30 minutes and drain. Chop the figs.

Preheat the oven to 180°C (350°F). Grease a 23 cm (9 in) round springform cake tin with butter and line the base with baking paper. Peel, core and slice the apples quite thinly. Immediately sprinkle them with the lemon juice.

Mix the polenta, flour, ground almonds, breadcrumbs, salt and soft light brown sugar together in a large bowl. Lightly beat the eggs and add the milk, honey, olive oil and orange-blossom water. Make a well in the centre of the dry ingredients and gradually pour in the wet mixture, mixing as you do so. Add the soaked dried fruit, apples and the citrus zests and scrape into the prepared tin. Bake for about 45 minutes. The cake should be coming away from the sides of the tin and a skewer inserted into the middle should come out clean. Leave in the tin for 20 minutes, then turn out onto a wire rack.

Carefully peel off the baking paper before serving and turn the right way up – the cake is fragile so be careful. Sift the icing sugar over the top. Serve with crème fraîche or whipped cream (if desired). The cake is best eaten lukewarm or at room temperature.

bread & crackers

OATMEAL & HONEY BREAD

Delicious, good for you and the quickest bread in the world to make, this is lovely with cheese and soup.

FROM THE GROCER

75 g (2¾ oz) cold butter, cut into little chunks, plus extra for greasing

175 g (6 oz) wholemeal (whole-wheat) flour

115 g (4 oz) plain (all-purpose) flour

1 teaspoon bicarbonate of soda (baking soda)

a pinch of salt

75 g (2¾ oz) super-fine oatmeal

25 g (1 oz/¼ cup) rolled (porridge) oats, plus extra for sprinkling

2 tablespoons soft light brown sugar

80 g (2¾ oz) runny honey

275 ml (9½ fl oz) buttermilk, plus extra if needed

white sesame seeds, for sprinkling

Preheat the oven to 180°C (350°F). Grease a 450 g (1 lb) loaf (bar) tin with butter.

Mix the flours, bicarbonate of soda and salt together in a large bowl and rub in the butter with your fingers. Add the oatmeal, oats and sugar and mix well.

Stir the honey into the buttermilk and add this to the flour mixture. Mix, using a wooden spoon or a blunt-edged knife, until the dough comes together. You might need a little more milk – if you don't have any more buttermilk, normal milk will do. Bring the dough into a ball with your hands and put it into the prepared tin. Press down lightly to fit and smooth the top. Sprinkle with oats and sesame seeds and bake for 45 minutes. Leave in the tin for 10 minutes, then turn out and leave to cool completely on a wire rack.

MULTIGRAIN & SEED LOAF

A good and solid plain loaf packed with grains and seeds.

FROM THE GROCER

3 teaspoons dried active yeast

1 teaspoon soft light brown sugar

sunflower or groundnut oil, for oiling

115 g (4 oz) malthouse flour

85 g (3 oz) strong white bread flour, plus extra for dusting

55 g (2 oz) rye flour

30 g (1 oz) rolled (porridge) oats

25 g (1 oz) polenta

1½ teaspoons salt

15 g (½ oz) butter, at room temperature

1 egg, beaten

oats, pumpkin seeds (pepitas), white sesame seeds and hemp seeds, for sprinkling

Put the yeast in 50 ml (1¾ fl oz) lukewarm water, add the sugar and stir well. Leave in a warm place for 15 minutes to 'sponge'.

Oil a 450 g (1 lb) loaf (bar) tin. Sift all the flours into a bowl, then put the bran collected in the sieve back into the bowl. Add the oats, polenta and salt and make a well in the centre. When the yeast has sponged, pour it into the well and then add the butter. Mix everything together with a wooden spoon or a blunt knife, and then start to bring the dough together with your hands. Slowly add about 125 ml (4 fl oz/½ cup) lukewarm water – you might need less or a little bit more – to form a soft dough. Knead for 10 minutes by hand or for 6 minutes in a mixer with a dough hook. Put the dough into a bowl and lightly oil all over. Cover with lightly oiled plastic wrap and leave somewhere warm to rise for 1 hour.

Preheat the oven to 200°C (400°F). Tip the dough onto a lightly floured work surface and knock it back for about 30 seconds. Form the dough into a loaf shape, drop it into the prepared tin and cover with lightly oiled plastic wrap. Leave somewhere warm to prove for 30 minutes, or until the dough has nearly doubled in size. Brush with the beaten egg – being careful not to let it drip down the sides of the tin – and sprinkle on the oats and seeds.

Bake for 30 minutes, or until the bread is golden brown and sounds hollow when you tap its underside.

DANISH SPELT, WHEAT & YOGHURT BREAD

This is a nice soft loaf with a good tangy flavour from the yoghurt.

FROM THE GROCER

18 g (¾ oz) dried active yeast

½ teaspoon soft light brown sugar

100 g (3½ oz) wheat grain (wheat berry)

200 g (7 oz/1⅓ cups) wholemeal (whole-wheat) flour

200 g (7 oz/1⅓cups) spelt flour

1 teaspoon salt

200 g (7 oz) plain yoghurt

1 tablespoon sunflower oil, plus extra for oiling

sunflower kernels, for sprinkling

Mix the yeast with the sugar and 80 ml (2½ fl oz/⅓ cup) lukewarm water, and leave somewhere warm for 15 minutes or so while it froths. Put the wheat grain in a saucepan with 250 ml (8½ fl oz/1 cup) cold water and bring to the boil. Reduce the heat to a simmer and cook, uncovered, for 15 minutes. Don't let the grain boil dry. Drain and reserve the cooking liquid – you should be left with about 50–75 ml (1¾–2½ fl oz). Tip the grain into a bowl and leave to cool.

Sift the flours and salt together and put the bran collected in the sieve back into the flour. Mix the yoghurt into the yeast mixture and pour this into the middle of the flour. Add the oil, the grains and the reserved cooking liquid. Gradually bring the dry ingredients into the wet ones and mix together with your hands until you have a soft dough. Add a little more water or flour as needed. Knead for 10 minutes by hand or about 6 minutes in a mixer with a dough hook. Place in an oiled bowl and roll the dough around to coat. Cover with oiled plastic wrap and leave somewhere warm for 1 hour, or until the dough has doubled in size.

Preheat the oven to 200°C (400°F). Lightly oil a baking tray. Knock the dough back for 30 seconds or so, form into a round loaf shape and place on the prepared baking tray. Cover with the oiled plastic wrap again and set aside somewhere warm until it has doubled in size. Brush the top with water and sprinkle on the sunflower kernels. Bake for 45 minutes. Test for doneness by sliding the bread off the baking tray and tapping it on the underside – the bread should sound hollow.

PUMPERNICKEL

This bread takes effort but you are rewarded with an incredible smell while it cooks – deep and yeasty with tones of coffee and chocolate. It's wonderful with smoked salmon and cured herring.

FROM THE GROCER

30 g (1 oz) dried active yeast

½ teaspoon soft dark brown sugar

30 g (1 oz) dark chocolate, broken into small pieces

1 teaspoon strong instant coffee granules

1 tablespoon treacle or molasses

125 g (4½ oz/½ cup) plain yoghurt

340 g (12 oz) rye flour

½ teaspoon soft light brown sugar

350 g (12½ oz/2⅓ cups) wholemeal (whole-wheat) flour, plus extra for dusting

1 tablespoon salt

1 teaspoon toasted caraway seeds, ground

55 g (2 oz) butter, melted and cooled

sunflower or groundnut oil, for oiling

1 egg white, lightly beaten

1 tablespoon caraway seeds, for sprinkling

1½ teaspoons white sesame seeds, for sprinkling

To make the starter dough, put 2 teaspoons of the yeast and 80 ml (2½ fl oz/⅓ cup) lukewarm water in a bowl and stir in the soft dark brown sugar. Leave somewhere warm for 15 minutes to 'sponge'. Put 300 ml (10 fl oz) boiling water into a bowl with the chocolate and stir until melted. Add the coffee and treacle, stir well, then add the yoghurt. Mix in the frothy yeast and 225 g (8 oz/2¼ cups) of the rye flour, cover with a clean tea towel (dish towel) and leave to stand overnight.

Mix the remaining 4 teaspoons yeast with 80 ml (2½ fl oz/⅓ cup) lukewarm water and the soft light brown sugar. Put this somewhere warm for 15 minutes.

Sift together the remaining 115 g (4 oz) rye flour and the wholemeal flour and put the bran that collects in the sieve into the bowl. Add the salt and ground caraway seeds. Make a well in the centre of the flours and add the starter dough from the previous day, the yeast mixture and the melted butter. Bring the dry ingredients into the well, working with your hands to mix everything together. Have 150 ml (5 fl oz) lukewarm water standing by and add enough to produce a soft dough. Knead for 6 minutes in a food with a dough hook or 10 minutes by hand.

Put the dough in a lightly oiled bowl and cover with oiled plastic wrap. Leave at room temperature for 2 hours 30 minutes, or until doubled in size. Dust a work surface with flour and knock back the dough for about 30 seconds, return to the bowl, cover and leave for another 2 hours 30 minutes.

Preheat the oven to 200°C (400°F) and lightly oil two baking trays. Divide the dough in half, shape each piece into an oval and place 1 on each baking tray. Cover with plastic wrap and leave to rise until the dough has nearly doubled in size. Brush with the egg white and sprinkle with the seeds. Slash the top of the loaves diagonally about 4 cm (1½ in) deep in four places. Bake for 15 minutes, turn the oven down to 180°C (350°F) and bake for 40 minutes. The loaves should sound hollow when tapped underneath when cooked. Move the loaves onto a wire rack to cool. They are delicious served with butter.

SCANDINAVIAN BARLEY FLATBREAD

This gives you fresh bread really fast. It has a distinctive barley taste and is good warm from the oven with sweet or savoury toppings. It's particularly delicious with smoked ham or salmon, or strong cheese.

FROM THE GROCER

175 g (6 oz) stoneground barley flour, plus extra for dusting

50 g (1¾ oz) malted bread flour

½ teaspoon salt

2 teaspoons soft light brown sugar

Preheat the oven to 240°C (465°F). Line a baking tray with baking paper.

Put the flours into a bowl and add the salt and sugar. Measure out 200 ml (7 fl oz) water and mix enough into the flour to produce a soft dough, but not one that is too wet. The dough should be soft and pliable. Knead lightly, then separate into 4 balls.

On a lightly floured work surface, roll each ball into a circle about 12 cm (4¾ in) in diameter. Don't worry about the thickness – if you roll them out to this size the thickness will be right. Slide onto the prepared baking tray and bake for 15 minutes. The flatbreads will be puffed up and slightly golden. Move to a wire rack and leave to cool slightly before eating.

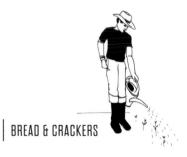

DATE, ORANGE & CHIA LOAF

Be prepared for a really addictive sweet bread – this is deep, sweet and fudgy tasting. Eat it spread with butter for afternoon tea.

FROM THE GROCER

175 g (6 oz) dried dates, pitted

50 g (1¾ oz) dried apricots

175 g (6 oz) butter, plus extra
for greasing

175 g (6 oz) soft dark brown sugar

1 egg, lightly beaten

100 g (3½ oz/⅔ cup) plain
(all-purpose) flour

125 g (4½ oz) wholemeal
(whole-wheat) flour

1 teaspoon baking powder

a generous grating of nutmeg

a pinch of ground cinnamon

50 g (1¾ oz/½ cup) pecans, roughly
chopped

1½ tablespoons chia seeds, plus
1½ teaspoons, for sprinkling

FROM THE GREENGROCER

finely grated zest of 1 orange

Put the dates and apricots into a saucepan and add 125 ml (4 fl oz/
½ cup) water. Bring to the boil, reduce the heat and simmer gently
for 15 minutes. Leave to cool in the water.

Preheat the oven to 180°C (350°F). Grease a 1 kg (2 lb 3 oz) loaf (bar)
tin with butter and line the base with baking paper. Melt the butter, let
it cool slightly, then add it to the dates and apricots. Mix in the sugar,
followed by the orange zest and egg.

Sift the flours together and put the bran in the sieve back into the flour.
Add the baking powder, nutmeg, cinnamon, pecans and 1½ tablespoons
of chia seeds. Make a well in the middle and add the date and egg mixture,
mixing in the dry ingredients with a spoon as you do so. Make sure
everything is completely combined. Scrape into the prepared tin and
sprinkle on the remaining chia seeds. Bake for 1 hour 15 minutes.
A skewer inserted into the middle should come out clean.

Leave to cool in the tin for 10 minutes and then turn out onto a wire
rack. Remove the paper and set the right way up. Leave to cool.

BEETROOT, CARROT & MULTISEED TEA LOAF

It's hard to believe beetroot (beets) and carrots are actually in this loaf. Add dried fruit or nuts to the batter if you like. Spread with butter and eat for afternoon tea or breakfast.

FROM THE GROCER

225 g (8 oz) butter, melted and cooled, plus extra for greasing

100 g (3½ oz/⅔ cup) plain (all-purpose) flour

100 g (3½ oz/⅔ cup) wholemeal (whole-wheat) flour

100 g (3½ oz/⅔ cup) wholemeal (whole-wheat) spelt flour

2 teaspoons bicarbonate of soda (baking soda)

a pinch of salt

1½ teaspoons ground cinnamon

1 teaspoon ground ginger

225 g (8 oz) soft light brown sugar

3 eggs, at room temperature

2 teaspoons natural vanilla extract

1 tablespoon each sunflower kernels and chia and pumpkin seeds (pepitas)

2 tablespoons poppy seeds, plus extra for sprinkling

FROM THE GREENGROCER

finely grated zest of 1 orange

115 g (4 oz) grated beetroot (beet)

115 g (4 oz/¾ cup) grated carrot

Preheat the oven to 170°C (340°F). Grease a 1 kg (2 lb 3 oz) loaf (bar) tin with butter and line the base with baking paper. Sift the flours together and put the bran in the sieve into the bowl. Mix in the bicarbonate of soda, salt, cinnamon, ginger and sugar.

Lightly beat the eggs together with the melted butter. Add the vanilla. Make a well in the centre of the dry ingredients and pour in the egg mixture. Gradually mix the dry ingredients into the wet ones. Add the orange zest, the sunflower kernels, the poppy seeds, the chia seeds, the pumpkin seeds and the grated vegetables.

Scrape the mixture into the prepared tin, sprinkle some poppy seeds on top and bake for 1 hour 15 minutes. A skewer inserted into the middle of the cake should come out clean when the loaf is cooked. Remove from the oven and let the loaf sit in the tin for 15 minutes, then turn out onto a wire rack to cool.

THIS is a super easy loaf to make and although the resting time is long, the delicious flavour will reward you for your patience. The quinoa flour gives it a distinctive taste and a nice soft crumb.

how to
MAKE A NO-KNEAD QUINOA LOAF

1 Sift 400 g (14 oz/2⅔ cups) wholemeal (whole-wheat) bread flour together with 100 g (3½ oz) quinoa flour and put the bran that collects in the sieve into the bowl. Add 1½ teaspoons salt and mix well.

2 Mix in 1 teaspoon fast-action yeast then pour in 470 ml (16 fl oz) warm water and stir until just combined into a very wet dough. Cover with plastic wrap and set aside to rest somewhere warm for 20 hours.

3 Gently tip the dough onto a lightly floured board and shape into a round loaf. Cover with a clean, damp tea towel (dish towel) and set aside for 2 hours to rise.

4 While the dough is rising, preheat the oven to 220°C (430°F) and place a heavy, lidded cooking pan in the oven.

5 When the dough has risen, carefully transfer it to the hot pan and sprinkle 2 tablespoons mixed seeds over the top of the loaf, pressing them in very gently. Cover and return to the oven.

6 Cook for 30 minutes then remove the lid and cook for 10–15 minutes more, or until golden on top. Tip out onto a wire rack to cool.

CARROT, ORANGE & PUMPKIN SEED BREAD

This makes slightly sweet bread that's delicious with cheese.

FROM THE GROCER

3 teaspoons dried active yeast

1½ tablespoons soft light brown sugar

110 g (4 oz/¾ cup) wholemeal (whole-wheat) spelt flour

110 g (4 oz/¾ cup) strong wholemeal (whole-wheat) flour

225 g (7 oz/1½ cups) strong white flour

1 teaspoon salt

100 g (3½ oz) pumpkin seeds (pepitas)

2 tablespoons sunflower kernels

1 tablespoon sunflower oil, plus extra for oiling

2 eggs, beaten

FROM THE GREENGROCER

grated zest of 1 orange

125 g (4½ oz) grated carrot

Put the yeast and ½ teaspoon of the sugar into a bowl with 60 ml (2 fl oz/¼ cup) lukewarm water. Stir and leave somewhere warm to 'sponge' for 15 minutes.

Sift the flours together and put the bran caught in the sieve into the bowl. Add the salt, the remaining sugar, 4 tablespoons of the pumpkin seeds, the sunflower kernels, orange zest and carrot. Make a well in the middle and pour in the frothy yeast, the sunflower oil and half the beaten eggs. Pour in 180 ml (6 fl oz) lukewarm water and mix the flour and carrot into the wet mixture. Bring together into a soft dough and knead for 10 minutes by hand or for 6 minutes in a mixer with a dough hook.

Put the dough into a lightly oiled bowl and cover with oiled plastic wrap. Leave somewhere warm until doubled in size.

Knock back the dough, shape it into an oval loaf and place on a lightly oiled baking tray. Cover with oiled plastic wrap and leave to prove until it is 1½ times its original size. Preheat the oven to 200°C (400°F). Brush the top of the dough with the remaining beaten egg and sprinkle the remaining pumpkin seeds on top. Bake for 35–40 minutes. Check for doneness by tapping it on the bottom – if the loaf sounds hollow then it's ready. Leave to cool.

SPELT, YOGHURT & PUMPKIN SEED ROLLS

Both tangy and sweet, these are lovely served warm at breakfast and also great with thick wintry soups.

FROM THE GROCER

18 g (¾ oz) dried active yeast

2 tablespoons soft light brown sugar

200 g (7 oz) plain yoghurt

200 g (7 oz/1⅓ cups) wholemeal (whole-wheat) spelt flour, plus extra for dusting

200 g (7 oz/1⅓ cups) white spelt flour

1½ teaspoons salt

sunflower oil, for oiling

1 egg, beaten

pumpkin seeds (pepitas), for sprinkling

Put the yeast, 50 ml (1¾ fl oz) lukewarm water and 1 teaspoon of the sugar into a bowl, stir well and leave somewhere warm for 15 minutes. Stir the rest of the sugar into the yoghurt and mix well.

Sift together the flours and salt, then put the bran collected in the sieve back into the flour. Make a well in the centre and pour in the yeast mixture, then the yoghurt. Mix with a wooden spoon or a blunt knife and bring the ingredients together with your hands to form a dough. Gradually add about 25 ml (¾ fl oz) lukewarm water – more or less as required – or more flour if the dough is too wet. Knead for 10 minutes by hand or 6 minutes in a mixer with a dough hook. Place in an oiled bowl, turning to coat, and cover with lightly oiled plastic wrap. Leave somewhere warm for 1 hour.

Preheat the oven to 200°C (400°F). Line a baking tray with baking paper. Lightly dust a work surface with flour and knock the dough back for about 30 seconds. Using floured hands split the dough into 10 little balls. Place them on the prepared baking tray, leaving space for the rolls to expand. Cover loosely with oiled plastic wrap and leave somewhere warm for about 30 minutes. Carefully brush the rolls with the egg and sprinkle over the pumpkin seeds. Bake for 30 minutes, or until golden, then remove from the oven and leave to cool on the baking tray. Once the rolls are cool enough to handle, move them onto a wire rack.

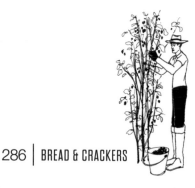

FIG & HAZELNUT BREAD

Don't chop the figs too much – you want to be able to slice through big chunks when you cut into the bread. That's why you leave the nuts whole too. This is great cheese bread.

FROM THE GROCER

75 g (2¾ oz) cold butter, cut into little chunks, plus extra for greasing

175 g (6 oz) wholemeal (whole-wheat) flour

75 g (2¾ oz) malthouse flour

115 g (4 oz) plain (all-purpose) flour

1 teaspoon bicarbonate of soda (baking soda)

50 g (1¾ oz) soft light brown sugar

175 g (6 oz) ready-to-eat dried figs, stems removed, cut into large pieces

100 g (3½ oz) blanched hazelnuts, left whole

275 ml (9½ fl oz) buttermilk, plus extra if needed

sunflower kernels and rolled (porridge) oats, for sprinkling

Grease a 1 kg (2 lb 3 oz) loaf (bar) tin with butter. Preheat the oven to 180°C (350°F).

Mix the flours, bicarbonate of soda and sugar together and rub in the butter with your fingers. Mix in the figs and the hazelnuts. Add the buttermilk and a little extra if necessary to form a consistent dough. Bring everything together with your hands and put it into the prepared tin. Smooth the top and sprinkle with the sunflower kernels and oats. Bake for 50 minutes.

Leave the loaf in the tin for 10 minutes, then turn out onto a wire rack. Turn it right side up and leave to cool.

RUSSIAN BLACK SEEDED BREAD

Dense, dark and delicious, this intensely flavoured bread works well with strong cheese and smoked salmon or cured herring. Breadcrumbs made from this bread when it goes stale are good for the Danish pudding Peasant girls in a mist (page 240).

FROM THE GROCER

2 teaspoons salt, plus extra for salting

1½ tablespoons black treacle (molasses)

3 teaspoons muscovado sugar

1½ tablespoons unsweetened (Dutch) cocoa powder

1 tablespoon instant coffee granules

4 teaspoons dried active yeast

125 g (4½ oz/1¼ cups) rye flour

200 g (7 oz/1⅓ cups) strong white flour, plus extra for dusting

225 g (8 oz/1½ cups) strong wholemeal (whole-wheat) flour

20 g (¾ oz) butter, melted and cooled

sunflower oil, for oiling

3 teaspoons caraway seeds

4 tablespoons mixed seeds such as pumpkin (pepitas), sesame, poppy, hemp, linseeds (flax seeds) and sunflower kernels

FROM THE GREENGROCER

170 g (6 oz) floury potatoes, peeled

To make the starter dough, cook the potatoes in lightly salted boiling water until tender. Drain and reserve 250 ml (8½ fl oz/1 cup) of the water. Mash the potatoes and push them through a sieve to make a smooth purée. Stir the treacle, 2 teaspoons of the sugar, the cocoa and coffee into the reserved water and mix well, then stir this mixture into the potato. Leave to cool until lukewarm, add 2 teaspoons of the yeast and the rye flour. Cover with plastic wrap and leave overnight.

The following day, put the remaining 2 teaspoons of yeast in a bowl with 60 ml (2 fl oz/¼ cup) lukewarm water and the remaining sugar, and leave somewhere warm to 'sponge' for 15 minutes.

Sift the strong white and wholemeal flours together with the salt and put the bran in the sieve into the bowl. Make a well in the middle and put the starter dough and the newly sponged yeast into it. Add the butter and pull the dry ingredients into the wet ones with your hands to make a soft dough. Lightly oil a work surface and your hands and knead the dough for about 10 minutes or 6 minutes in a food fitted with a dough hook. Transfer to a lightly oiled bowl and cover with oiled plastic wrap. Leave to rise until almost doubled in size, about 1 hour 30 minutes.

Knock back the dough on a lightly floured work surface. Combine the caraway seeds and the mixed seeds and put all but 1 tablespoon into the dough. Knead briefly to incorporate the seeds and shape the dough into a round loaf, smoothing it nicely and tucking the seam underneath. Place on a lightly oiled baking tray. Cover with oiled plastic wrap and leave to prove for about 1 hour.

Preheat the oven to 200°C (400°F). When the dough has proved, remove the plastic wrap; brush the top with water and sprinkle over the remaining 1 tablespoon of seeds. Bake for 30 minutes, then check for doneness – the bottom should sound hollow if you tap it. If it doesn't, return the loaf to the oven and cook for another 5 minutes or so.

OATCAKES

These are softer and more buttery than regular Scottish oatcakes.

FROM THE GROCER

125 g (4½ oz) wholemeal (whole-wheat) flour

250 g (9 oz/2 cups) medium-ground oatmeal

125 g (4½ oz) plain (all-purpose) flour, plus extra for dusting

½ teaspoon bicarbonate of soda (baking soda)

1 teaspoon salt

½ teaspoon caster (superfine) sugar

250 g (9 oz) cold butter, cut into cubes

1 medium egg, beaten

Mix all the dry ingredients together in a bowl. Rub in the butter until you have a mixture that looks like breadcrumbs. Add the egg and bring everything together into a dough using your hands. Wrap the dough in plastic wrap and chill for 30 minutes. Preheat the oven to 180°C (350°F).

Lightly dust a work surface with flour, roll the dough out thinly and stamp out biscuits (cookies) using a 6 cm (2½ in) plain round cutter. As you cut out the biscuits lay them on a baking tray lined with baking paper. Cook for 15–18 minutes. The biscuits should look slightly toasted but not at all brown. They will become firm as they cool – don't try to move them before then.

RYE CRISPBREADS

These are much more delicious than any crispbread you can buy and incredibly quick to make. Ring the changes by scattering them with whatever seeds you like.

FROM THE GROCER

250 g (9 oz/2½ cups) rye flour, plus extra for dusting

1 teaspoon salt

1 teaspoon soft light brown sugar

½ teaspoon baking powder

25 g (1 oz) cold butter, cut into little cubes

150 ml (5 fl oz) full-cream (whole) milk

Preheat the oven to 200°C (400°F). Lightly flour a non-stick baking tray – you may need more than one if it's on the small side.

Put the flour, salt, sugar and baking powder into a bowl and rub in the butter with your fingertips. Using a blunt knife mix in the milk, then use your hands to pull everything together into a soft dough. The dough will be sticky but don't panic – it will get easier to work with. Resist adding more flour.

Lightly dust a work surface with flour and roll chunks of the dough into very thin, irregular rounds, trimming into squares if desired. These need to be thinner than any pastry you have ever made – thinner than you can measure. As you form each crispbread, transfer it to the prepared baking tray. When you have used up the dough, prick a few holes in each crispbread with a fork. Bake for 10 minutes but keep an eye on them – crispbreads burn easily.

Transfer the crispbreads onto a wire rack as soon as you can handle them and leave to cool. Eat, as the Scandinavians do, with cured herring, smoked salmon, herbed sour cream and cheese.

AMERICAN CORN BREAD

This has a cakey rather than a bread-like texture and is delicious crumbled into a salad of bacon, tomatoes and spring onions (scallions).

FROM THE GROCER

2 tablespoons sunflower or groundnut oil

125 g (4½ oz) corn kernels, frozen or tinned

150 g (5½ oz/1 cup) polenta

15 g (½ oz) plain (all-purpose) flour

2¼ teaspoons baking powder

1 teaspoon bicarbonate of soda (baking soda)

¼ teaspoon salt

1 tablespoon soft light brown sugar

1 egg, beaten

170 ml (5½ fl oz/⅔ cup) buttermilk

15 g (½ oz) butter, melted

FROM THE GREENGROCER

4 spring onions (scallions), chopped

2 small red chillies, halved, seeded and thinly sliced

Preheat the oven to 210°C (410°F). Oil a 20 cm (8 in) round cake tin with 1 tablespoon of the sunflower oil and place in the oven. The tin needs to get very hot before you pour in the corn bread batter.

Heat the remaining oil in a frying pan over a medium heat and sauté the spring onions, chillies and corn (drained if tinned) for 1 minute.

Sift all the dry ingredients together into a bowl. Mix the egg and the buttermilk together in a pitcher. Make a hollow in the middle of the dry ingredients and gradually pour in the buttermilk mixture, stirring and bringing in the wet ingredients as you do so. Add the melted butter and the spring onion mixture.

Very carefully take the cake tin out of the oven and pour in the batter – it should sizzle a little. Bake for 15–20 minutes until the bread is golden on top and the edge is starting to come away from the side of the tin. Turn the bread out onto a wire rack to cool.

A note on these recipes.

Eggs are large unless stated otherwise.
If not specified, butter should be salted.

Index

Acknowledgements

Thanks to everyone who worked on this book and made it beautiful: Alice Chadwick for her lovely design, Amelia Wasiliev for her top-notch cooking and styling, and Deirdre Rooney for the great photos. And Sue Quinn, my editor, was a joy to work with, not least because she loves and understands food as well as words.

First published by Marabout (Hachette Livre) in French in 2013.

This edition first published in 2013 by Hardie Grant Books
Paperback edition published in 2016

Hardie Grant Books (Australia)
Ground Floor, Building 1
658 Church Street
Richmond, Victoria 3121
www.hardiegrant.com.au

Hardie Grant Books (UK)
5th & 6th Floors
52–54 Southwark Street
London SE1 1UN
www.hardiegrant.co.uk

All rights reserved. No part of this publication may be reproduced, stored in a retrieval system or transmitted in any form by any means, electronic, mechanical, photocopying, recording or otherwise, without the prior written permission of the publishers and copyright holders.

The moral rights of the author have been asserted.

© Hachette Livre (Marabout) 2013
43 Quai de Grenelle, 75905 Parais Cedex 15

A Cataloguing-in-Publication entry is available from the catalogue of the National Library of Australia at www.nla.gov.au
Grains
ISBN 978 1 74379 216 2

Design and illustration: Alice Chadwick
Photography: Deirdre Rooney
Food styling: Amelia Wasiliev